CIVIL WAR IN CONNACHT

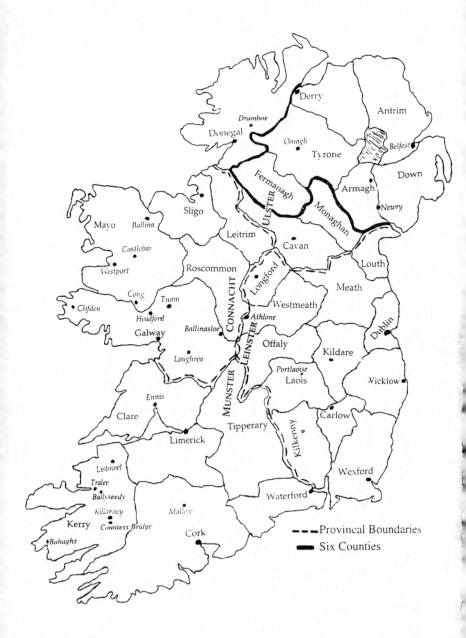

CIVIL WAR
IN
CONNACHT

NOLLAIG Ó GADHRA

MERCIER PRESS

MERCIER PRESS
PO Box 5, 5 French Church Street, Cork
16 Hume Street, Dublin 2

Trade enquiries to CMD DISTRIBUTION,
55a Spruce Avenue, Stillorgan Industrial Park, Blackrock, Dublin

© Nollaig Ó Gadhra, 1999

ISBN 1 85635 281 1

10 9 8 7 6 5 4 3 2 1

Dedication

TO ALL THOSE WHO MADE SACRIFICES
IN THE INTERESTS OF IRISH FREEDOM

Printed in Ireland by Colour Books Ltd.

CONTENTS

Introduction

THIS BOOK IS BASED SUBSTANTIALLY on a series of notes which *The Tuam Herald* editor, David Burke, asked me to compile to mark the seventy-fifth anniversary of the Civil War. In this part of the country the Civil War was most poignant at the very end, when six Republicans were executed on Wednesday 11 April 1923 in the old workhouse in Tuam. I was reluctant to give a blow by blow account of the lead-up to that sad and tragic event, even if I do feel we should honour, remember and pray for those noble souls now and in the future. But it is also necessary to try and set these events in some sort of context.

I decided to give this account a somewhat local Galway flavour, to draw extensively on notes compiled a quarter of a century ago, at the time of the fiftieth anniversary, by J. J. Waldron of Tuam, in honour of John Henehan, Athenry Road, Tuam – 'in memory of the days we roamed together on two wheels on the dusty road from Annaghdown Castle to Ballycurran Castle, Co. Galway'. These notes were completed in October 1972 – at a time when far more survivors of the Civil War were around than today – and those who lived through the events would demand right of reply.

My aim was to try and establish a record, as compiled by the late J. J. Waldron of Tuam, and to add whatever national or historical context that would make the book a useful resource for students in the future. Thanks are due in particular to the editor of *The Tuam Herald* for allowing a mere outsider (who was not even born in Connacht) so much space and latitude. It is typical of the record of fair and balanced service to the entire Connacht community, for which provincial papers like *The Tuam Herald* have been famous for generations. They have set, and indeed continue to set, an example for our national media, and even for our as yet young local electronic media.

While this account focuses largely on the perceptions of J. J. Waldron in Tuam and the surrounding areas, one of the other reasons why West Galway/Connemara features less prominently is that the area was merged with West Mayo as part of the Fourth Western Division of the IRA – west of the line from Ballina to An Spidéal. This does not mean that I am not happy to include a reference, for example, to the two volunteers, Lt Thomas James and Capt. Pat Morrison, who were killed in an attack on the Marconi station outside Clifden on 29 October 1922. These two names are not normally read out in the Galway Roll of Honour because they were both Mayomen. They were taken back to their native area and buried in the Republican Plot in their local cemetery in Ballina. I am deeply grateful to Mary Lysaght, Margaret Joyce and all those who filled me in on this part of the story. Thanks, too, to Hugh Ginty, Ballina, Co. Mayo.

I am aware that the full story of the Civil War in Connacht, or the west of Ireland, has been tailored to some extent in this book because I have placed the emphasis on the Waldron notes from *The Tuam Herald* series. I realise that further stories need to be told, for example, about the work of Liam Mellows, the organiser for the Irish Volunteers in Galway, and the west, from as early as 1915 and the impact this had on the decision to mount the biggest mobilisation outside Dublin in 1916, eastwards of the city. There is also an essay by Edward Gallagher on how 'Thirty IRA Men Defied 600 British Troops at Tourmakeady' on 3 May 1921 based on an account by Tom Maguire, OC South Mayo Brigade which proves that largescale confrontations with crown forces were no longer confined to the southern counties in the months before the Truce of 11 July 1921. I hope this book, with a different geographic and personality emphasis, will add to our knowledge of the fight for freedom in Connacht.

I am grateful to the retired teacher in Tuam who filled me in on the activities of the Special Branch in Galway in the years after the Civil War was over, and indeed into the 1930s, when the De

Valera government inherited the political control of the elaborate state machine, already under the control of the late Peter Berry, who served in the Department of Justice from Kevin O'Higgins in 1927 to Desmond O'Malley in the early 1970s. Berry made anti-Republican 'subversion' his speciality and his role was as crucial in the late 1920s, before Fianna Fáil gained office in 1932, as it was at the time of the Arms Crisis of 1969–70. Berry believed state security was far too important to be left to fickle politicians and his legacy and the system he operated is a matter which should be fully investigated if we want to know the full truth of the legacy of the Civil War.

Thanks are also due to my many advisors who put me right on various specific points while working on this book. While they are too numerous to mention individually, a special word of thanks needs to be extended to the relatives of the people involved who gave me use of family material, including copies of the last letters written by some of the men the night before they were executed in January and April 1923 – in Athlone and Tuam.

Many of the letters to *The Tuam Herald* about the series came from America – sad, realistic insights into the horror of war, any war, but especially civil war. These letters were typical of what happened to many families in the first decade of 'freedom' as the new Free State tried to work with the limited independence they had won, in an increasingly complex world. For example, Charles O'Donnell wrote as follows: 'My mother, Maria Blake O'Donnell, a widow with nine children, operated a shop and public house where we lived. The soldiers arrived in the evening and a number came to our shop and served themselves.

'I was a ten year old, and I was in the kitchen doing my homework, and two soldiers were assigned to the kitchen. They were guarding a Lewis 75 machine-gun that they had brought into the kitchen. A number of other soldiers were in the shop.

'Suddenly two men, armed with pistols, came into the kitchen and ordered the two soldiers up against the wall, disarmed them and took the Lewis gun. I understand that others confronted the soldiers in the shop.

'Like any sensitive and sensible ten-year-old, I was frightened and ran upstairs to where my mother was tending to one of my sisters, Molly, who was very sick. I remember my mother being very upset with the commotion, and I can still picture her wringing her hands. She did this all too frequently, since it was very difficult, trying to run her husband's shop after he died in 1919, and to raise nine children. Finally, in about 1928, she could no longer continue in business, and by 1930, all of the O'Donnells had migrated to America.'

It was mainly to America that Irish people in economic difficulties, and Irish Republicans in particular, turned. These Republicans were denied jobs at home by the people who came into power on the backs of the sacrifices many Republicans had made in the freedom struggle on the basis of political discrimination. It was not unlike the politics of exclusion practiced by Stormont against Catholics, Nationalists and Republicans in the six counties who were ensnared in the totally arbitrary and sectarian Northern Irish state, even though many had fought to liberate the whole country.

There was also an email from Michael J. Donlon of Staten Island, New York. Michael, a native of Dunmore, Co. Galway, brought me an important document – a collection of prisoners' autographs collected by a relative of his while in jail for the Republic in Maryboro Jail [now Portlaoise]. There are no Galway names in the book – most of those who wrote their verses and did their little drawings, in the spring of 1923, were from Dublin, Wexford and other parts of the south-east and midlands. The book is in very good condition, having spent more than seventy-five years in New York, and Michael Donlon would like to present it to the Irish nation and to Irish Republican scholarship. I would like to suggest that all county councils and other local authorities set about establishing local museums or archives where such material could be deposited – not stacked away in some basement of the National Library, Museum or Archive in Dublin where, naturally, there is only room for the national story of our struggle for freedom to be on permanent display above ground.

I want to thank everyone who encouraged or helped me in any way with the preparation of this book. It proved to be a more complex and frustrating undertaking than what one normally encounters in undertaking a localised historical 'slice of life' and trying to set it in some sort of national context for today's readers. Special thanks are due to the library staff in National University of Ireland, Galway and my colleagues in GMIT for various bits of research and references; to the staff of *The Tuam Herald*, and especially the editor David Burke; to those involved with the publication of *Eleven Galway Martyrs*, produced by Councillor Frank Glynn and his Commemoration Committee at the time of the Tuam Workhouse monument unveiling in 1985; to the local media who co-operated in my many public appeals for specific items or information; and to the many people who gave permission to reproduce copyright material. I would, finally, like to thank my wife, Máirín, and my family, for listening to the stories, again and again, as I was writing and researching the material for this book. A huge big 'míle maith agaibh' for the patience, tolerance and insights which the questioning last word, by sharp minds, can produce.

NOLLAIG Ó GADHRA
21 JANUARY 1999

Rialtas Sealadach na h'Eireann

———•———

The members of Rialtas Sealadach na h'Eireann received surrender of Dublin Castle at 1.45 p.m. to-day.

It is now in the hands of the Irish Nation.

For the next few days the functions of the existing departments of that Institution will be continued without in any way prejudicing future action.

Members of Rialtas Sealadach na h'Eireann proceed to London immediately to meet the British Cabinet Committee to arrange for the various details of handing over.

A statement will be issued by the Rialtas Sealadach na h'Eireann to - morrow in regard to its immediate intentions and policy.

For Rialtas Sealadach na h'Eireann
(Signed) MICHAEL COLLINS,
Chairman.

January 16, 1922

Backdrop

ANY OTHER CIVILISED COUNTRY IN the world would mark 21 January 1919 – the founding of the First Dáil Éireann – as our real Independence Day. Even in the context of the Civil War those who claimed in 1992–23 that 'what was good enough for Mick Collins is good enough for me' need to be reminded of the blood, sweat, tears and lives which Collins, Cosgrave, Mulcahy, Fitzgerald, Blythe, Hogan, MacNeill, O'Duffy and the rest were prepared to sacrifice throughout 1919, 1920 and 1921 to ensure the survival of the First Dáil and the Irish Republic.

When the great divide came, as J. J. Waldron wrote in his notes, the Galway situation was complicated because the line between the First Western Division (Clare/South Galway) of the IRA and the Second Western Division (South Roscommon, South and East Mayo, North Galway) ran more or less along the railway line from Galway to Athlone. The First Western Division under Commandant Michael Brennan, was pro-Treaty, while the Second, under Commandant Thomas Maguire, was anti-Treaty, pro-Republican. Brennan was an exception along the west coast. Maguire, as we know, became a legend over a long lifetime, by refusing to compromise, even after Dev had broken with Sinn Féin and taken his new Fianna Fáil party into the Free State Dáil in 1927. The influence of the local IRA commanders was the key factor in influencing the Volunteers in 1922, not the elected politicians like De Valera. The influence of the secret IRB organisation, then headed up by Michael Collins, was crucial. In a video interview I did with General Maguire on the seventieth anniversary of the founding of the First Dáil, in 1989, when Tom was a bright and articulate 97 years of age, he recalled how pressure was brought to bear on all the back-bench TDs in the Second Dáil, by Collins' IRB men to vote for the Treaty. When they arrived in Dublin for the vote, they were met at the railway station and told that each and every member would have to speak in the Treaty debate and publicly declare their position. Tom, who was against the Treaty, would not be moved or bullied and said so. When I suggested that I had not seen his speech in the debate and that it must have been a very short one, he agreed, it was. Two words: 'Ní toil.'

Because these IRA Divisions, and the people who led them, are crucial to any understanding of the state of the country in 1922–23, I will list them here as quoted by J. J. Waldron from Eoin Neeson's book, *The Civil War in Ireland:*

MARCH 1922 – IRA DIVISIONS

First Northern: Donegal, Four Brigades, Commdt Joseph Sweeney, *Pro-Treaty.*

Second Northern: Tyrone and Derry, Four Brigades, Commdt Charlie Daly, *Anti-Treaty.*

Third Northern: Belfast, Antrim, North Down, Commdt Joseph McKelvey, *Anti-Treaty.*

Fourth Northern: Armagh, West and South Down, North Louth, Commdt Frank Aiken, *Anti-Treaty.*

Fifth Northern: Monaghan, East Cavan and South Fermanagh, Commdt Dan Hogan, *Pro-Treaty.*

First Eastern: Meath, Westmeath and Kildare, Nine Brigades, Commdt Seán Boylan, *Pro-Treaty.*

Dublin No. 1: Commdt Oscar Traynor, *Anti-Treaty.*

South Dublin Brigade: Commdt Andrew MacDonnell, *Anti-Treaty.*

North Wexford: North Wexford and South Wicklow, Commdt Joseph Cummin, *Pro-Treaty.*

South Wexford Brigade: Commdt Thomas O'Sullivan, *Anti-Treaty.*

Carlow Brigade: Commdt Liam Stack, *Pro-Treaty.*

Midlands Division: Longford, Leitrim, Fermanagh, Commdt Seán MacEoin, *Pro-Treaty.*

First Western: Clare and South Galway, Commdt Michael Brennan, *Pro-Treaty.*

Second Western: South Roscommon, South and East Mayo, North Galway, Commdt Thomas Maguire, *Anti-Treaty.*

Third Western: North Roscommon, Sligo and part of East Mayo, Commdt Liam Pilkington,* *Anti-Treaty.*

Fourth Western: North and West Mayo, parts of Sligo and Galway, Commdt Michael Kilroy, *Anti-Treaty.*

First Southern: Cork, Kerry, Waterford, West Limerick, Ten Brigades, Commdt Liam Lynch, *Anti-Treaty.*

Second Southern: Kilkenny, Limerick and part of Tipperary, Five Brigades,

Commdt Earnán O'Malley, *Anti-Treaty.*
Third Southern: Laois, Offaly, part of Tipperary, Five Brigades, Commdt
    Michael McCormack, *Pro-Treaty.*

*In later life Fr Liam Pilkington. Unlike most of the other commanders of the period, who chose
careers in the army or in politics, Pilkington went on to become a priest as soon as his services in
the cause of the Republic had come to an end.*

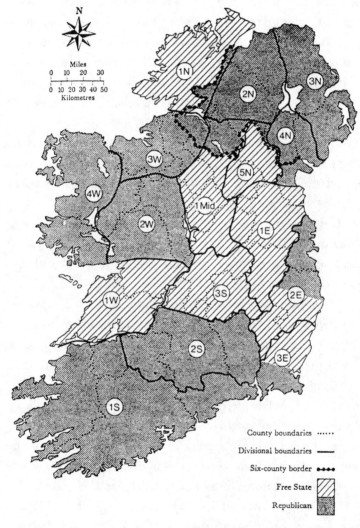

Map source: *Green against Green, The Irish Civil War,* Michael Hopkinson, Gill
and Macmillan, Dublin 1988.

Rory O'Connor, Interview and Letter

Writing in 1972 under the general heading 'The Civil War' Mr Waldron said: 'The first book published on *The Civil War in Ireland* was issued in 1966. The author was Eoin Neeson. This is not a detailed history; it gives the particular phases of the Pro and Anti-Treaty movements to the climax of the ceasefire when the order was given by Frank Aiken on May 4th, 1923. A Safety Act was passed by the Dáil in June 1923 and we know from present day experiences what that implied. A general election was mooted for August 27th 1923 and in the election the Pro-Treaty party had a majority. Neeson asks how men who had just spent four years as comrades in arms, fighting side by side against the British, came to turn the guns on one another? It is quite evident that both sides made tragic blunders.

'Neeson thinks that perhaps one important point that may have had a bearing on the delegation that met Lloyd George to discuss the Treaty was that they were already divided in opinion to such an extent that they travelled in two groups by different routes when going to London.

'A member of the Provisional Government of the period named Blythe, who is still with us (1972), has made the following statement re the civil war: "All countries must have civil war, social or political, in their evolution, and the sooner the better". In my notes I only give what the public were told of the day to day actions between the Free State troops and the Republicans and probably the former's point of view.

'So to get the opposite point of view, an attempt should be made before it is too late to collect all information from the members still alive of those who took part in the war of 1922–1923.

'The beginning of the Civil War came about with the kidnapping of General J. J. O'Connell, Assistant Chief-of-Staff of the National Army, on June 26th, 1922. He was held prisoner in the Four Courts where the Republicans had their headquarters.

'At midnight on June 27th an ultimatum was delivered to the Four Courts demanding an end to the occupation. When the time limit had elapsed the National Army proceeded to bombard the building. The operation was carried out by the officers and men of Longford Brigade.

'The decision to bombard the Four Courts was not taken on orders from Churchill as is often said. The government decided to take action after careful consideration over a period, i.e., a favourable election result and the detention of General O'Connell, brought the issue to a head.'

There follows part of an interview given by Rory O'Connor to Mrs Clare Sheridan before the bombardment. Waldron says 'Mrs Sheridan was well-known in Galway in later years. She lived at the Spanish Arch and carried on her crafts there of artist and sculptor.' The interview was written for and published in the *The New York Times:*

'Mrs C. S. to R. O'C.:
'I asked him if he believed he could make a successful Republic if he had it in his hands?
'"Yes," he replied. "I don't see why a Republic shouldn't be easily a success. I don't dream of an Ireland smoking with chimney stacks, I don't think factories bring good conditions of happiness, but we could be a very prosperous rural people and could afford to buy what ships we need for our export."
'At that moment the telephone bell rang and from what I could make of the one-sided conversation he must have been answering a press representative.
'He said, "No it is not customary to answer speeches of any British ministers, they may say what they like, it makes no difference, what is that? They are going to blow us out of here? Just say that when they come we are ready for them," and he rang off.
'I said, "Surely you will not stay here? They will blow the wall and roof down on your head, you haven't an earthly chance."
'He shrugged his shoulders, "then I will go down in the ruins or flames," he replied.
'When he said goodbye we looked at one another intently but did not speak our thoughts, I felt I was shaking hands with a man about to die. Alone, I made my way back across the courtyard to the gate.

'A ragged crowd as seen in a French Revolutionary film [was] gazing through the bars. They made way for me to pass out and watched me wonderingly as I walked the quays by the Liffey. To one looking back at this beautiful building with its central copper dome and its defaced sand-bagged windows, they seemed a heroic little band of rebels in the midst of a world of opposition.

'In a few days the sequel was revealed. The Republicans were attacked but did not suffer many casualties, the civil authorities were the chief victims of the fight, as most of the records in the building were burned. Rory O'Connor did not go down in the ruins or flames and when finally an explosion filled the sky with fragmentary documents, Winston Churchill philosophically told the British people that "a state without Archives is better than Archives without a state".

'(Mrs Sheridan was a cousin of Churchill and whenever her name appeared in a paper it was always tagged with his name, as if that matter-ed a thrawneen to us Irish.)'

LETTER FROM RORY O'CONNOR
Sent from Mountjoy Prison, Dublin, August 1922

The lies and hypocrisy of the Free State leaders are astounding, especially to those of us who took part in the army negotiations for unity and who know the whole inner history of those negotiations.

We were never requested to evacuate the Four Courts. On the contrary, at one meeting of the Coalition Army Council, at which Mulcahy, O'Duffy, Mellows, Lynch and myself were present, we were only asked to evacuate the Ballast Office, the Kildare St Club, the Masonic Hall and Lever Bros.

At that stage we actually discussed co-ordinated military action against NE Ulster and had agreed on an officer who would command both Republican and Free State troops in that area. We were also to send from the south some hundreds of our rifles for use in that area. The reason given was that it would never do if rifles which had been handed to the 'Government' for use against the Republic, and which of course, could be identified, were found in use against Craig. An exchange of rifles was effected. It should be remembered that at this time the 'Government' was publicly declaring that it was the mutineer section of the army that was fighting the Ulster people.

At this meeting I have referred to, someone suggested the evacuation of the Four Courts, and Mulcahy laughingly said that as long as we held the place the war against NE Ulster would be attributed to us. We, of course, had no objection. From this you will see the real reason why we were not asked to evacuate the Four Courts.

THE 'PACT' ELECTION
16 JUNE 1922

I HOPE TO SKETCH THE atmosphere in Tuam in the summer of 1922 as the clouds of civil war began to spread out from Dublin after the capture of the Four Courts by the pro-Treaty forces of the Provional Government. They set out to 'capture the country' during the crucial months of July and August 1922, when no Dáil of any sort, Republican or Provisional, was in session. The 'Provisional Parliament' to which the Provisional Government, established according to the British interpretation of the 1920 Government of Ireland Act, would be responsible, was prorogued no less than five times. By the time this 26-county chamber was finally brought together in Leinster House on 9 September 1922, the main moulds of the new Free State were already emerging.

Down the country the real 'dual-power' conflict arose as the British forces withdrew from the 26 counties, and the old armed police force, the RIC, or what was left of it, was disbanded. This meant there was immediate competition between local Republican and pro-Free State troops to take over the barracks being evacuated. Tuam and Galway were no exception.

But before proceeding to examine the specifics of the dual-power situation that existed in July/August 1922, it is necessary to spell out the details of the Collins–De Valera Pact which was agreed on 20 May 1922 – a mere few weeks before the outbreak of hostilities in Dublin. These are the pact details:

We are agreed:
1 That a National Coalition panel for this Third Dáil representing both parties in the Dáil and in the Sinn Féin organisation be sent forward on the ground that the national position requires the entrusting of the government into the joint hands of those who have been the strength of the national situation during the last few years, without prejudice to their present respective positions.
2 That this Coalition panel be sent forward as from the Sinn Féin organi-

sation, the number from each party being their present strength in the Dáil.

3 That the candidates be nominated through each of the existing party executives.

4 That every and any interest is free to go up and contest the election equally with the National–Sinn Féin panel.

5 That constituencies where an election is not held shall continue to be re-presented by their present deputies.*

6 That after the election the executive shall consist of the President, elected as formerly; the Minister for Defence, representing the army; and nine other ministers – five from the majority party and four from the minority, each party to choose its own nominees. The allocation [of office] will be in the hands of the President.

7 In the event of the Coalition government finding it necessary to dissolve, a general election will be held as soon as possible on adult suffrage.

* To accommodate representation in the six north-eastern counties.

Because the collapse of this pact agreement led to civil war in the middle of 1922, it is perhaps appropriate to spell out some of the lesser-known facts about this arrangement – essentially the first attempt at cross-party consensus and coalition government in the Irish democratic model of the emerging PR elections.

After the overwhelming Sinn Féin victory in the December 1918 election, held under the British straight-vote model, the British government – realising there was no way of recovering any ground – decided to allow PR for elections in Ireland. They were, however, careful not to introduce PR for their own elections in England, Scotland and Wales, or for elections to the imperial parliament in Westminster – the national parliament as they saw it.

A new and, at first encounter, a fairly complicated PR system of single transferable vote in multi-seat constituencies was included in the Government of Ireland Act 1920. It also provided for two separate elections, to two separate 'internal parliaments' – one in Belfast for six of the nine counties of Ulster, and the other in Dublin in which Leinster, Munster, Connacht and the three Ulster counties of Donegal, Cavan and Monaghan only could be represented. This partition legislation, for which no MP from Ireland had voted, was pushed through Westminster two days before Christmas on 23 December 1920. While elections were generally contested in the six partitioned counties in May 1921 under this act, no polls were held in the other twenty-six counties which were fighting the Black and Tan war. All members – 124 Sinn Féin and 4 Unionists [for Dublin University, Trinity College graduates were allocated 4 seats] – were returned unopposed. The Sinn Féin members let it be known that they regarded their mandate to be that of TDÉ [Teachta Dála Éireann] to the Second Dáil Éireann in which deputies from the six severed Ulster counties could also sit. This Second Dáil came together in August 1921.

The Second Dáil voted in favour of the Articles of Agreement [The Treaty] – signed on 6 December 1921 – by 64 votes to 57 on 7 January 1922. But the British insisted, in accordance with their interpretation of the act, and as provided for in the Articles of Agreement, that the Treaty be ratified, again, by the pro-Treaty TDs and the Trinity College Unionists – drawn only from the twenty-six counties – at a once-off meeting of 'the parliament of Southern Ireland' in the Mansion House, Dublin, on 14 January 1922. It was only having gone through these motions that the British handed over control of Dublin Castle to Michael Collins as chairman of a new Provisional Government on 16 January 1922.

Because the members of the Second Dáil were returned unopposed in May 1921, the June 1922 Pact election was the first time that most Irish voters had to use the complicated PR voting system. Little attention has been paid to this fact and to the historic 'Pact Election' which was held in the 26 counties on 16 June 1922. This was the election which had been promised by Griffith and Collins ever since they pushed the 1921 Treaty, with IRB pressure, through the Second Republican Dáil Éireann on 7 January 1922. The people were to give their verdict in this June 1922 election, allegedly, after they had considered the realities of the Treaty proposals as set out in a new draft constitution for the Irish Free State. Everybody admits that Collins in particular tried to get as much as possible out of the Treaty settlement in the course of drafting the proposed new constitution, during the first months of 1922. But Churchill, as colonial secretary, and the British government insisted that there would be no going back from the essential compromises of Irish sovereignty conceded in the Treaty itself. Thus the oath remained, the new 26 county Dáil would be convened by the governor general, acting on behalf of the crown, and Northern Ireland would have to be recognised even if the exact nature of the border would be decided by a Boundary Commission at a later date. As it happens the actual draft of the Free State constitution was not published until the morning of the poll itself, 16 June 1922. This meant, in a pre-radio age, that the vast majority of voters outside Dublin, in any case, had no opportunity to examine what was on offer.

The poll was seriously flawed in other ways also. The electoral register was a number of years out of date and had not been reviewed because of the troubled state of the country during the Black and Tan period. Women between the ages of 21 and 30 were still excluded from voting, as they had been under British law in 1918. Given that all six women in the Second Dáil Éireann voted against the Treaty, and the Volunteer generation [under 21] who had been caught up in the revolution, could not vote, it seems that the odds were against the anti-Treatyites in this Pact Election. But the poll is more significant in that it marked the first attempt by the new Sinn Féin political elite, which seized power in the historic 1918 general election, to initiate something like 'power-sharing' or 'coalition government' by consensus, so that the deep divide that split the nation after the Treaty was signed, without being referred back to Dublin, would not descend into Civil War.

The famous 'Pact' from which the election gets its name was signed by Éamon de Valera and Michael Collins on 20 May 1922. The Second Dáil Éireann wound up business on 6 June 1922 for the duration of the election, due to be held on 16 June. The Republican

Second Dáil was due to be re-convened on 30 June 1922, when a new Third Dáil would be summoned by the Ceann Comhairle of the outgoing Republican chamber. In order to prevent the Sinn Féin representatives of that Second Dáil from tearing each other apart in the election campaign, Collins and De Valera had agreed a Pact that would work for a consensus and that would be reflected in the form of a 'National Coalition' as soon as the new Dáil assembled. The product of three days of negotiation, between the Long Fellow and the Big Fellow, the main idea was the brainchild of Harry Boland who was annoyed that similar ideas which he proposed some months earlier had not been accepted at the time, before the bitterness intensified. The 'Pact' provided for a national coalition of outgoing Sinn Féin candidates in proportion to the numbers, pro and anti-Treaty, in the outgoing Second Dáil. Non-Sinn Féin candidates would also be free to stand, including Labour and Farmers' parties, who had stood aside in 1918 and 1921 in order to maintain the national consensus in favour of Sinn Féin in its struggle against the British. After the election a Sinn Féin National Coalition Government of nine members would be formed with a membership of five to four, depending on which side got the most votes on the Treaty issue. In other words, Sinn Féin supporters were being asked to back candidates on the basis of their stand on the Treaty, but the promise of a consensus national government was provided for, in order to prevent the Republican movement from splitting. The Sinn Féin members of the Second Dáil Éireann would choose the various panels of candidates in every constituency. Both sides in that Second Dáil welcomed the Collins–De Valera Pact. An extraordinary Ardfheis of Sinn Féin also endorsed it rather than take some harsh decisions.

It must have been clear, for example, that since all the 'other' new candidates would be pro-Treaty, the possibility of Republican Sinn Féin people getting a good result was slim before other difficulties arose. The Treaty was not referred to in the Pact, but it was agreed that if the promised coalition broke down, there would be another general election. Arthur Griffith opposed the Pact idea, because, he argued, it did not allow the people to judge the issue of the Treaty itself. The British were appalled, because they suspected, the Pact, if honestly operated, would enable the growing Republican sentiment against the Treaty to express itself. And if the people voted for the Free State compromise, the pro-Treaty Sinn Féiners were committed to having four anti-Treaty voices out of the nine in the new coalition arrangement.

As soon as it became clear that pro-Treaty people won most of the seats in the Pact Election, Collins and his friends in the Provisional Government put the idea of a power-sharing coalition with De Valera's Sinn Féin out of their mind. Collins, in particular, seems to have realised that the Pact would not work, if only because it was in breach of Article 17 of the Treaty which said that every member of the new government would have to accept the Treaty in writing (see pp. 175–176).

When nominations closed on 6 June 1922, it emerged in the 26 counties that only in seven constituencies were the Panel candidates (pro-Treaty and anti-Treaty) unopposed. The Unionists, representing Trinity College, were unopposed also, but in the remaining 20 constituencies they were opposed by the Labour Party, the Farmers' Party and Independents.

At first the election campaign was agreed with Pact candidates sharing platforms and addressing meetings in common. Collins and De Valera both spoke at the opening meeting in Dublin's Mansion House on 9 June 1922. But within a few days things changed. Collins went to London on the night of 12 June – four days before the election. He met Churchill, the colonial secretary, the following day and returned to Cork on 14 June 1922. Here he made a speech, widely reported, which directly repudiated the Pact. He said: 'You are facing an election here on Friday and I am not hampered now by being on a platform where there are coalitionists. I can make

ELECTION POSTER, 1922
Issued by the Pro-Treaty Party before the 'Pact' election

You can get the Republic for all of Ireland through the safe and sure method of the Treaty or you can try another round through the alphabet of miseries.

A	Auxiliaries
B	Black and Tans
C	Commandeering
D	Deaths
E	Executions
F	Fatalities
G	Gallows
H	Hangings
I	Internments
J	Jails
K	Knoutings
L	Licence
M	Murders
N	Nerve Strain
O	Oppression
P	Persecution
Q	Questionings
R	Raids
S	Spies
T	Threats
U	Usurpation
V	Vandalism
W	Wails
XYZ	The final horrors which words cannot describe

To get (perhaps) document No. 2.

VOTE FOR THE TREATY

a straight appeal to you – the citizens of Cork – to vote for the candidate you think best of ... When I spoke in Dublin I put it as gravely as I could that the country was facing a very serious situation. If the situation is to be met as it should be met, the country must have the representatives it wants. You understand fully what you have to do and I depend on you to do it.' *The Freeman's Journal* printed headlines in large type drawing attention to the significance of the Collins speech. 'After such a speech the Pact can only be described as breaking up' commented the *Daily Mail*.

The final outcome of the election was announced on 24 June 1922 and two divergent views were taken of the result immediately. Of the Panel candidates 94 had been returned, 58 pro-Treaty and 36 Republicans. The pro-Treaty group had been reduced from 66 to 58, the anti-Treaty group had been reduced from 53 to 36, not counting Seán O'Mahony who, in accordance with the provisions of the Pact, was to retain his Fermanagh/Tyrone seat – a symbolic link with the six counties that reminded everybody of the real significance of partition. Labour won 17 seats, Farmers 7. There were 4 Unionists representing Trinity College and 6 Independents. In summary:

Pro-Treaty	58
Anti-Treaty	36
Labour	17
Farmers	7
Unionists	4
Independents	6
Total	128

Of the 620,000 votes cast (a turnout of just less than 60%), 229,193 went to pro-Treaty Sinn Féin candidates (58 seats), 133,864 voted anti-Treaty (36 seats) and some 247,276 voted for non-Pact candidates who were nearly all pro-Treaty (34 seats). Farmers' Party candidates were successful in all but one of the constituencies they contested, while the Labour Party gained 29.4% of the vote to take 17 seats. In all, more than 78% of the poll had voted to support the Treaty, and while we have touched already on some of the factors which distorted this result against Republicans, few can doubt the influence of this victory on decisions taken in the weeks immediately afterwards.

The decision to send in the Free State troops against the Four Courts on 28 June 1922 – two days before the Second Dáil Éireann was due to re-assemble on 30 June 1922 – was a turning point. In fact the Provisional Government proclaimed the coming together of the Third All-Ireland Dáil Éireann due on 30 June 1922. The Dáil was prorogued for over two months while the Free State army, after the Four Courts surrender, went after Republican positions in the west and the south. The new Third Free State Dáil, open only to TDs from 26 counties, and bound by oath to the British crown, did not finally assemble until 9 September 1992. By then the Civil War was a bloody reality but the 'cleaning up', to force a Republican surrender with so much evil and bitterness until the spring of 1923, had still to be endured.

On 22 June 1922 Field Marshal Sir Henry Wilson, former Chief of the Imperial General Staff, was shot dead outside his London house by two Irish men. Wilson, born in Co. Longford was a most influential Irish Unionist, with a distinct hatred for all things pertinent to Irish independence. He was considered responsible for the pogroms against the Catholic nationalist minority in Belfast. In 1920 he had objected to unauthorised reprisals carried out by British troops only because: 'If these men [IRA and civilians] ought to be murdered, then the government ought to murder them.'

It has been generally accepted that the killing of Wilson was carried out by order of Michael Collins. The two Irishmen who were captured on the spot (and hanged a few weeks later) were Collins' own men. Collins' motives still remain obscure. The consequence was that the British immediately chose to blame the IRA, in particular the garrison holding the Four Courts buildings in Dublin.

Other important moves were also afoot, though these probably went largely unnoticed down the country. For example, the Supreme Court of the Irish Republic which had functioned under Dáil Éireann law since 1920, in peace and war, and which could not, in theory, be dismissed without a solemn resolution of two-thirds of the total membership of the Dáil, was now 'suspended' by proclamation of 'the Cabinet of An Dáil' even though no Dáil sat during these months. On 20 July 1922 the Provisional Government revoked its stated intention to establish courts of law and equity and criminal jurisdiction and because of this, the Foreign Affairs Minister George Gavan Duffy, a distinguished lawyer, resigned in protest.

Two senior Republican TDs Cathal Brugha, Minister for Defence (7 July) and Harry Boland (2 August) were killed in this period. In August 1922, pro-Free State TD, Arthur Griffith died on 12 August and Michael Collins was killed in the Béal na mBláth ambush on 22 August 1922. These events shocked the nation, but it should be remembered that the first two TDs to be shot were Republicans.

RELEASE THE
PRISONERS!

There are 15,000 Prisoners in Goal : ROTTING.

You know what they are suffering. If you don't ask their relatives.

Many of their relatives are literally : STARVING.

There are in Kilmaniham Gaol alone 500 Girls. HOW MANY DID ENGLAND PUT IN GAOL?

Hunger-strike after hunger-strike had taken place in these bastilles in an attempt by the prisoners to lessen the sufferings of those among them whom they know to be unable to bear their privations.

KNOW THE TRUTH despite the Censor's gag of the past twelve months.

These men have suffered in the gaols of TWO "governments."

HAVE YOU NO GRATITUDE?

Release the Prisoners.

STAND-OFF IN TUAM
JULY – AUGUST 1922

THE WALDRON NOTES GIVE A wonderful insight into the continuing 'stand-off' situation that prevailed in Tuam as in other areas in the west of Ireland, during the summer months of July and August 1922. These were the months when the Provisional Government, still unwilling to call together the Provisional Parliament to which they said they were to be responsible, pursued their main war effort against the south. In places like Tuam the stand-off continued as is clear from the following factual reports and Waldron notes:

July 1st, 1922
Much uneasiness is felt through the country at the differences between the Pro- and Anti-Treaty followers. Many are hoping that better counsels would prevail. People generally await the outcome of the struggle with restrained anxiety and all are hoping that through mediation or some good counsel, peace may again be possible.

July 8th, 1922
Tuam, although completely in the hands of the Republican forces since the Civil War began, was peaceful. To the credit of the local commandant, be it said, order was well-kept and with the exception of one unfortunate contretemps [accident] there were no disturbances. Although goods were commandeered from several shops in town, receipts were given. Immediately there was [a] sign of the railway closing down, a rush was made on the provision shops to procure supplies. Some not content with their supplies sought selfishly to capture more. This move was countered by Commandant Dunleavy who saw to it that supplies were evenly distributed and in one case a person seen carrying away two bags of flour was

made to return one. A rumour went the rounds that the barracks, and Cloonmore and Grange bridges were to be blown up, but there was no truth in the rumours.

The old RIC barracks in Tuam were vacated during the week by its former occupants. The latter were followers of the anti-Treaty party and there were rumours around the town that the Free State troops were coming along to take possession of the workhouse soon, to use it as a military barracks.

July 15th, 1922

A sensation was caused in Tuam on Thursday when it was mooted that brigade officers and about 40 men of the Fourth Western Division had resigned. No reasons were given for the resignations. When the police vacated the local police barracks some months ago a local man, Commandant Dunleavy, was placed in charge there and had been brigade commandant for the district up to the unfortunate split in the army.

He and his staff officers joined the Republican forces and have since held the Tuam barracks and calm and quietness have reigned over the area during their occupation. Commandant Dunleavy and his two brothers were on active service up to the Truce in July last (1921).

July 29th, 1922

On the morning of July 25th the Free State army marched into Tuam and took over the workhouse as their military barracks. It wasn't a pleasant morning to be on the road; as a matter of fact it was raining cats and dogs all night and the troops, 70 of them, were like drowned rats after marching all night. They had a hard time also removing the barricades they met with on the road.

The last of the English forces had left the barracks about six months previously, they were the King's Own Yorkshire Light Infantry. They had a jolly good time in Tuam, the only untoward incident during their stay was the execution of one of their privates for disposing of parts of a gun to a party in a Headford pub. He was court-martialled in Headford and executed in England.

The forces on their departure from Tuam, headed by their band, marched around Ballymote, came down Bishop Street on the way to the station to entrain, and kept step to the tune 'Marching through Georgia'.

Castlegrove House was burned down on July 25th, the residence of Mr Tom Lewin. The IRA were in occupation there after leaving Tuam barracks. They have disclaimed responsibility for the burning and it is rumoured that the act was an agrarian affair.

An Interlude

We hear that Waterslade was the scene of great excitement on Tuesday evening when a young man was seen rushing over the bridge on Shop Street shouting 'They're coming, they're coming! Hurrah!' The relief of Lucknow was nothing to it! Several of the inhabitants rushed out on the street, to see what it was all about, thinking the Free State army, perhaps, had arrived, but they were evidently not in the know. The young man ran so recklessly that he ran over a poor man's ass tied to a telegraph pole at the corner and bumped straight into the 'Mahdi' [Islamic heroic figure] putting this six foot six and 20-stone body sprawling on the ground. Fortunately, the Mahdi's rotund body just rolled along the ground and saved him from serious injury. He had a few bruises all right, but when some Zam Buk [popular ointment] was applied they all disappeared.

The man with the mutton head was the cause of it all. He could not restrain himself anyhow when he realised that the 'Brown Stuff' had arrived from Galway at last, the only road open for supplies. So when he saw the two cart loads coming down Shop Street he had to give vent to his feelings of gladness, because soon his thirst would be quenched. The Micawber [Dickensian character in

33

Pickwick Papers who was always in debt] of the gang was the only sensible man in the crowd that night. He recited the 'Gander [poem/ditty]' in spirited style and everyone was so happy, forgetting the present troubles and of course the Mahdi forgot his ailments as well by the time he had let down two pints of his favourite Sarsparilla. If the relief had not come so opportunely, there would have been many cases for the county home that evening.

August 1st, 1922

At 10 o'clock on Tuesday morning Quartermaster J. J. Coakley of the Free State forces in the workhouse, Tuam, whilst in Dempsey's Butcher Shop in High Street ordering supplies, was suddenly surrounded by armed men and told to put up his hands. He did not comply with the order and was knocked down, disarmed and placed in a waiting car on the street.

The car then proceeded at a hot pace through Belclare and Caherlistrane and on arriving at Mossfort it broke down. The captive and his guards then walked to Headford where they commandeered a lorry and drove to the ferry at Lough Corrib where a boat was procured. The captive and the six men crossed to the other side in the direction of Oughterard. After landing on the other side of the lake, they came to rest in a small village. Whilst the party were chatting near a farmhouse, one of the guards produced a bottle of poteen which Coakley was asked to share, but he declined. One of the men said 'he could drink two bottles of the poteen without getting drunk'. It was stated, as a result of a bet made by Coakley, that the man could not accomplish what he boasted he could, four bottles of poteen were produced and the six men proceeded to consume the contents.

The effort proved too much for them and after a brief period, we are told, they departed to the land of Morpheus. In due course Coakley made his escape to Galway where he reported to the commanding officer of the Free State barracks and was driven back to his headquarters in Tuam none the worse of his adventure.

Mr Coakley was formerly an assistant in the establishment of Messrs M. S. Walsh & Sons of High Street, Tuam. He was active in the cause during the period of the Black and Tans and was arrested. Afterwards, when released, he went on the run.

A younger brother of his in Claremorris was accidentally shot whilst in the barracks after the Treaty.

August 8th, 1922

The Pavilion of the Tuam Golf Club at Cloonascragh was burned on Tuesday night, August 8th, 1922. The burning was blamed on the Republicans but their OC Con Fogarty issued a notice to the effect that they were not responsible. Many of those burnings at this period had an agrarian purpose, not military.

Perhaps the largest raid made so far by the Republicans on the town of Tuam took place on Saturday night. It was actually the first time that some members of both sides came to hand grips.

They appeared suddenly on the streets with rifles, searched a number of people and ordered them along with unarmed soldiers into the ruins of the burned town hall. A man named Pappy Whyte was driving a motor car down Vicar Street, when he was called upon to halt. Instead of doing so he put up speed even when shots were fired after him and escaped without injury. There were several Free State officers in the area dressed in civvies, and on hearing the shots, went to investigate. Two of them went in the direction of Canny's ruins and were immediately challenged to put their hands up. They refused to comply, there were three other men behind them with rifles, so they were in a very dangerous situation. One of the officers made a grab for the rifle held by the man nearest to him. In the course of the struggle, a shot went off, grazing the officer's hand and a second shot passed by his chin but still the struggle went on between the two combatants, both being evenly matched. They next found themselves across the road at Stafford's [now Kilgarriff's] hall door when the officer with great exertion pushed his assailant from him and getting inside the hallway pulled out his revolver and fired several shots onto the street. His attacker returned the fire, smashing Stafford's window, after which he retreated to join his comrades.

Whilst this was happening the other officer, taking advantage of the excitement caused by the noise of the shot, drew his revolver against the other assailant who, thinking he was being attacked from the rear, retreated and took cover successfully despite some shots being fired after him.

The officer then made for his barracks and secured extra men. Suspecting that some of the Republicans might be hiding in the old graveyard, the officer brought his men down High Street and shots were fired into it. There was no return fire so they continued their search around the Mall to Vicar Street. On coming to Whyte's corner they noticed a motor car without lights or occupants. They approached it cautiously and on searching it found inside a high explosive substance with a battery attached. Hearing footsteps they immediately took cover behind the car and noticed three men and rifles approaching. The officer called out 'who goes there?' and a voice replied 'friend' and also gave his name (apparently the speaker was left to guard the car).

The officer answered 'You are the man I want' at the same time firing his revolver. It suddenly dawned on the riflemen that they were conversing with soldiers of the Free State army so they beat a hasty retreat. In the meantime, the soldiers drove the car to Walshe's yard nearby to recover it later.

In their raid on the town the Republicans kidnapped an armed Free State soldier and brought him along when they retreated. Apparently, when some distance from the town they received word that the troops were in pursuit of them so they placed their captive into a farmhouse with instructions not to leave there until 8 a.m. next morning.

The common report afterwards was that the real objective of the raid was to draw the Free State troops from their barracks, as the Republicans had a large force stationed near the railway line on the Dublin Road opposite the military barracks, waiting for the opportunity to attack in order to release some prisoners held inside.

Forces of Provisional Parliament Advance
September – October 1922

Nationally the months of September-October 1922 were marked by the establishment of the new 26-county Dáil – or 'Provisional Parliament of Southern Ireland' on 9 September 1922.

There followed work on the preparation of a Free State Constitution, strictly in accordance with what Britain agreed were the limits of the Treaty. This was due to come into force, without a referendum, but by an act of the new UK parliament, on 6 December 1922. 'The Dáil' as the Pro-Treaty deputies had the honesty to call this chamber, in order to distinguish it from Dáil Éireann, also passed Emergency Powers legislation, which handed over the power to inflict the death penalty to a military tribunal, rather than the cabinet or a court of law.

A 'last chance' amnesty was declared in October, and in November 1922 the execution of 'rank and file' IRA members began in Dublin, on 17 November when Peter Cassidy, John Gaffney, James Fisher and Richard Twohig were shot 'for possession of revolvers without proper authority' on the day that the infamous trial of Erskine Childers began. In the new Leinster House Dáil consisting of less than 60 Pro-Treaty TDs, with Labour and Independents, General Mulcahy pleaded 'military necessity' in general terms.

Kevin O'Higgins made it clear that they had to 'take average cases' for the first executions. 'If we took some man who was outstandingly active ... the unfortunate dupes throughout the country might say that he was killed because he was a leader, because he was an Englishman, or because he combined with others to commit raids.' Clearly, this was a reference to Childers, then on trial for his life for possession of a Colt pistol, which ironically, had been given to him for his personal security by Michael Collins during the Treaty negotiations a year earlier. Childers became the fifth of the famous 77 'official executions' by the government during the Civil War. He was executed on 24 November 1922 while his case was still awaiting an appeal to the High Court.

THE HEIGHTENING TENSION IN THE Tuam area during the autumn months of 1922 is reflected in the Waldron notes, which begin with the following:

September 9th, 1922

Two sections of the National Army were ambushed near Tuam on Friday evening when Volunteer Walsh was killed and Volunteer Cooney wounded. The casualties on the Republican side are not known but traces of blood were seen in the area and men were seen carrying bodies through the fields afterward. Whether they were wounded or dead is not known.

Five motor loads of the army, travelling from Mountbellew to Tuam, stopped on the road at Lissavalley and dismounted within two feet of a land mine. Two officer members of the company named Lohan and Leahy placed their men [on] each side of the road and immediately fire was opened on them by the Republicans who had been concealed behind some walls. There was a brief exchange of shots when the Republicans were seen to be retreating. They were following the army for some distance when the commanding officer of the Republicans was captured with two of his men. A second mine was discovered and Brigadier General Fogarty and his two men were compelled to remove it from its position. The body of Volunteer Walsh was then conveyed to Tuam but on the way the party was ambushed. The troops took cover but after 20 minutes crossfire, the Republicans seemed to be retreating, leaving behind a pair of field glasses, an overcoat and ten rounds of ammunition. There were some important documents found on Fogarty; the other articles captured in the first ambush were two bicycles, one belonging to the post office, two coils of wire, one Mauser Rifle, revolvers and ammunition.

On Friday night last (9th) some young men with picks and crowbars completely demolished what was left of Cloonmore Bridge outside Tuam on the Galway road.

It had been blown up the week before and left with a gaping hole in the centre – a death trap across the road, but now there is nothing left.

The local people protested against its destruction and said 'the Black and Tans, as bad as they were, never did that'. They got little heed, some shots were fired over their heads and [they] were peremptorily ordered indoors.

September 12th, 1922

On Sunday last as the National Troops were searching the Ballinasloe area, coming to Clonbrock they surrounded a house there and learned that Republicans had been there, and beat up the occupant, an ex-policeman named Scully and took away his bicycle. The troops followed the trail of the bicycle which led to a gamekeeper's house on the estate. The call on those inside to come out with their hands up was met with a hail of bullets, coming thorough the windows of the house. The troops took cover and returned the fire. Ultimately, a member of the attacking force named Goode, an old IRA man, rushed the door and went into the kitchen and opened fire on those inside. After about a score of shots had been fired a prominent Republican named Jack Keogh walked from the house carrying a Webley revolver in each hand fully loaded. There was also found in a search of the house a new service rifle.

Jack Keogh was in charge of the [Republican] forces when the Free State forces were bombed in Ballinasloe some time ago, when one of their killers was killed and three wounded. He was the leader of the Republicans in South Galway.

Also captured with Keogh was J. Downey of Ahascragh who

had escaped from Portumna some time previous and an O'Neill of Tuam who had seen service since the Black and Tan times.

The troops' full haul was three bicycles, three service rifles, two Webley revolvers, fully loaded and 12 large bombs.

FR HEANEY, CC, AT MASS on Sunday, denounced the theft of timber from the Headford locality. He also availed of the occasion to refer to the action of certain girls in the area who he heard were carrying dispatches from camp to camp for the Republicans. He said parents should exercise proper control over their children and conduct of this kind above all.

September 16th, 1922

Mr Con Fogarty, OC of the IRA, Western Division, who was taken in an ambush a week from when Volunteer Walsh was killed, was removed from Tuam to Athlone. He was arrested amongst others in Tuam in 1920 by the crown forces and interned in Ballykinlar until the Truce. When released he joined the IRA unit and was in Tuam police barracks since its take over. After the resignation of Commandment Dunleavy he was appointed in his place and held command until the approach of the Free State army when they evacuated the barracks.

Due to the intervention of Most Rev. Dr Gilmartin, the IRA left without burning the barracks which Fogarty said was in contravention of orders from his headquarters. But he acceded to the archbishop's request, because there was a danger the fire would spread to adjacent houses.

Beside the barracks, too, were the ruins of Canney's Drapery, burned by the crown forces in 1920.

In the town during the week the National Army were on the alert for a surprise attack by the Republicans and searched all cars entering the town and ordered all public houses in Tuam to close at 9.30 p.m. each evening, under pain of a fine of £20.

September 20th, 1922

On Thursday night between 8 o'clock and 9 a large force of Republicans made a lightning attack on the town of Tuam. It was calculated that there had been three or four hundred of them, supposedly under the command of Commanders Maguire and Powell. They poured into town from all directions on cars, bicycles and on foot. They held up all pedestrians and made prisoners of all the Free State soldiers they met with. These were herded into the nearest halls and houses and deprived of their leggings and other equipment on them. Then an attack was made on the workhouse barracks, one from the racecourse and the other on the Dublin road, above the barracks. The attack was replied to vigorously by the garrison. The incessant firing was kept up for two hours and now and again one heard a heavy detonation, probably a bomb; firing died down only to be resumed again with less intensity. At about 2.30 a.m. all was quiet again and the Republicans took their departure not before they had visited several houses in the town and carted away a lorry load of supplies without much regard of the owners' feelings. Members of the various clubs were held inside rooms while the shooting lasted, and as firing died down they were allowed to go home. In all the excitement and shooting there were no casualties except for the terror inspired amongst the women and children. Planks were commandeered from a business house in town to place over the damaged Cloonmore Bridge so that vehicles could be hauled over it. Prominent citizens were said to be brought along but released later. Next day a mine and ammunition was found outside the workhouse wall.

September 23rd, 1922

On Saturday night an attempt was made on the life of the sentry at the Tuam workhouse barracks. Several shots were fired at him and some lodged in the wall very close to him. The troops rushed to the barrack gate where two men were observed running away; they gave pursuit. For three miles that was kept up, the Republicans turning at frequent intervals to fire at their pursuers. Nearing bogland the men endeavoured to lead the troops to a dangerous part but were unsuccessful. But eventually they themselves were in difficulties, and had to comply with the order of 'Put them up!' They surrendered and were arrested. They were found in possession of loaded Webley revolvers.

September 30th, 1922
It was reported that there were some disturbances among the political prisoners held in Galway Jail.

October 7th, 1922
A proclamation was issued by the Free State government offering a pardon and amnesty to all in arms against the state and who delivered up the weapons in their possession, and ceased to take part in armed opposition on or before October 15th, 1922.

The notice was made up of four explanatory paragraphs and signed – Liam T. MacCoscraigh (President of Dáil Éireann).

SURPRISE RAID
Another surprise raid was made by Republicans on Tuam on Saturday night last. About 36 of them took part, appearing in the streets of the town about 9 o'clock, holding up any pedestrians they came across and searching them for arms, then allowing them to pass on.

Some of the riflemen then proceeded to several shops and commandeered goods. The whole proceedings were carried out with clock-like precision; only one or two shots were fired. When they were satisfied with their seizures, they left the town taking with them two motor-cars. One, however, was returned that night.

Rumour says the prime object of the visit was to search for particular members of the Free State army. The next day, Sunday, typewritten notices signed by General T. Maguire, Second Division, were posted on the pillars at the cathedral entrance warning persons who repaired bridges or removed barricades, that they would be fired on. The notices also threatened any persons giving information to the National Troops about the movements of the Republicans. On Wednesday last Cahergal and Grange Bridges were destroyed. They were only repaired the week previous. Vehicles travelling from Tuam to Athenry to catch the Dublin train, will now have to take the longest way round, as the shortest way home. The bridge destroyers must get 'fed up' sooner or later with the futility of their efforts at self-destruction.

October 14th, 1922

After next Sunday the Army Council will begin to exercise the powers conferred on them by the government by setting up military courts. By regulations made on October 2nd, certain offences are punishable by death, penal servitude, imprisonment, internment or fines according to the nature of the offence.

The amnesty expires the same day that these regulations went into force.

October 29th, 1922

This week it was reported that Commandant Tom Maguire of the Western Brigade was captured with some of his men around Ballinrobe.

Mr P. Dunleavy, Tuam, who was captured (kidnapped) some weeks ago has escaped whilst in the custody of the Republicans. He was well treated and moved from place to place and in a different house each night. His brother Tim was also kidnapped, but was released after a hunger strike of some days.

Pro-treaty Army Council Proclamation, 10 October 1922

[Issued on 10 October 1922, after Special Emergency Powers were granted to the Provisional Government's army]

To All Whom it May Concern:

1. With a view to the speedy termination of the present state of armed rebellion and insurrection, and the restoration of peace, order and security, the Government with the sanction of Dáil Éireann, has sanctioned the doing by, under the authority of the Army Council, of all of the following matters or things:

(a) The setting up of Military Courts or Committees for the inquiring into charges against persons in respect of any of the offences hereinafter mentioned, provided, however, that every such Military Court or Committee shall include as a member thereof at least one person nominated by the Minister of Defence and certified by the Law Officer to be a person of legal knowledge and experience.

(b) The inquiry by such Military Courts or Committees into the cases of persons charged with any of the offences following, that is to say:

(1) Taking part in, or aiding or abetting any attacks upon or using force against the National Forces.

(2) Looting, arson, destruction, seizure, unlawful possession, or removal of, or damage to, any public or private property.

(3) Having possession without proper authority of any bomb, or articles in the nature of a bomb, or any dynamite, or gelignite, or other explosive substance, or any revolver, rifle, gun or other firearm or lethal weapon, or any ammunition for such firearm.

(4) The breach of any general order or regulation made by the Army Council.

and the infliction by such Military Courts or Committees of the punishment of death or of penal servitude for any period or of imprisonment for any period or of a fine of any amount either with or without imprisonment on any person found guilty by such Court or Committee of any of the offences aforesaid provided that no such sentence of death be executed except under the counter signature of two members of the Army Council.

(c) The removal under authority of the Army Council of any person taken prisoner, arrested, or detained by the National Forces to any place or places within or without the area of jurisdiction of the Government, and the detention or imprisonment of any such persons in any place or places within or without the area aforesaid.

(d) The regulation and control of the sale, possession, transfer of, and dealing in, revolvers, rifles, guns and other firearms.

2. By regulations made the 2nd day of October, 1922, the Army Council have provided for the trial by Military Courts of civilians charged with the offences specified in the preceding paragraph and for the infliction upon any civilian convicted by a Military Court of any such offence, of any of the following punishments according to the nature and gravity of the offence:

DEATH,
PENAL SERVITUDE,
IMPRISONMENT,
DEPORTATION,
INTERNMENT,
FINE.

3. It is provided by the said regulations that they shall come into force upon and shall apply as from such date as the Army Council shall determine and announce by proclamation.

4. By proclamation published the 3rd day of October, 1922, the Government announced and proclaimed as follows:

    (1)   Every person who is engaged in such insurrection and rebellion against the State as aforesaid, or in such armed opposition to the National Forces as aforesaid, or who has been guilty of any offence against the State, directly arising out of such aforesaid, and who, on or before the 15th day of October, 1922, voluntarily delivers into the possession of the National Forces all firearms, arms, weapons, bombs, ammunition and explosives, and all public and private property, now unlawfully in his possession, and quits all lands or buildings unlawfully occupied by him, and who, on or before the 15th day of October, 1922, voluntarily ceases to take part in, or aid or abet, such insurrection, rebellion, or armed opposition, shall be permitted to return unmolested to his house; and to every such person we hereby offer, assure and proclaim a full amnesty and pardon for all such insurrection, riot, rebellion, and opposition and offence as aforesaid.

    (2)   Every such person may deliver any such firearms, arms, weapons, ammunition, explosives and bombs, and any such public property as aforesaid, to the Officer Commanding the nearest Military position or Station, or to any such person as shall be nominated by him.

KNOW THEN, AND IT IS HEREBY ANNOUNCED AND PROCLAIMED AS FOLLOWS:

(1)   After the 15th day of October, 1922, we, the Army Council, will exercise all the powers and do all the matters and things in the first paragraph of this proclamation mentioned, or any of them, according as the same shall to us seem necessary or expedient.

(2)   The said Regulations as to the Trial of Civilians by Military Courts made by us, the Army Council, on the 2nd day of October, 1922, shall come into force and apply as from the 15th day of October, 1922.

Given at General Headquarters, Portobello Barracks, Dublin, and published this 10th day of October, 1922.

Signed on behalf of the ARMY COUNCIL.
RISTEÁRD UA MAOLCATHA, General,
Commander-in-Chief.

Catholic Pastoral Letter – October 1922

[Letter by Cardinal Logue and the archbishops and bishops read in all the churches and public oratories at the principal masses on Sunday 22 October 1922, i.e., a week after the implementation by the Free State Army Council of its draconian powers over life and death. Few doubt that this hierarchy support for Provisional Government gave the green light for the executions that began in November 1922]

Dear Rev. Father and Beloved Brethren,

The present state of Ireland is a sorrow and a humiliation to its friends all over the world. To us, Irish bishops, because of the moral and religious issues at stake, it is a source of the most painful anxiety.

Our country, that but yesterday was so glorious, is now a byword before the nations for a domestic strife, as disgraceful as it is criminal and suicidal. A section of the community, refusing to acknowledge the government set up by the nation, have chosen to attack their own country as if she were a foreign power. Forgetting apparently, that a dead nation cannot be free, they have deliberately set out to make our Motherland, as far as they could, a heap of ruins.

They have wrecked Ireland from end to end, burning and destroying national property of enormous value, breaking roads, bridges, and railways; seeking, by an insensate blockade, to starve the people, or bury them in social stagnation. They have caused more damage to Ireland in three months than could be laid to the charge of British rule in so many decades.

They carry on what they call a war, but which, in the absence of any legitimate authority to justify it, is morally only a system of murder and assassination of the National Forces – for it must not be forgotten that killing in an unjust war is as much murder before God as if there were no war. They ambush military lorries in the crowded streets, thereby killing and wounding not only the soldiers of the Nation, but peaceful citizens. They have, to our horror, shot bands of these troops on their way to Mass on Sunday; and set mine traps in the public roads, and blown to fragments some of the bravest Irishmen that ever lived.

Side by side with this woeful destruction of life and property there is running a campaign of plunder, raiding banks and private houses, seizing the lands and property of others, burning mansions and country houses, destroying demesnes and slaying cattle.

But even worse and sadder than this physical ruin is the general demoralisation created by this unhappy revolt – demoralisation especially of the young, whose minds are being poisoned by false principles, and their young lives utterly spoiled by early association with cruelty, robbery, falsehood and crime.

Religion itself is not spared. We observe with deepest sorrow that a certain section is engaged in a campaign against the bishops, whose pastoral office they would silence by calumny and intimidation and they have done the priesthood of Ireland, whose services and sacrifices for their country will be historic, the insult of suggesting a cabal amongst them to browbeat their bishops and revolt against their authority.

And, in spite of all this sin and crime, they claim to be good Catholics, and demand at the hands of the Church her most sacred privileges, like the Sacraments, reserved for worthy members alone. When we think of what these young men were only a few months ago, so many of them generous, kind-hearted and good, and see them now involved in this network of crime, our hearts are filled with bitterest anguish.

It is almost inconceivable how decent Irish boys could degenerate so tragically, and reconcile such a mass of criminality with their duties to God and to Ireland. The strain on our country for the last few years will account for much of it. Vanity, and perhaps self-conceit, may have blinded some who think that they, and not the nation, must dictate the national policy. Greed for land, love of loot and anarchy have affected others, and they, we regret to say, are not a few. But the main cause of this demoralisation is to be found in false notions on social morality.

The long struggle of centuries against foreign rule and misrule has weakened respect for civil authority in the national conscience. This is a great misfortune, a great drawback, and a great peril, for a young government. For no nation can live where the civil sense of obedience to authority and law is not firmly and religiously maintained. And if Ireland is ever to realise anything but a miserable record of anarchy, all classes of her citizens must cultivate respect for and obedience to the government set up by the nation, whatever shape it takes, while acting within the law of God.

This defect is now being cruelly exploited for the ruin, as we see, of Ireland. The claim is now made that a minority are entitled when they think it right, to take up arms and destroy the National Government. Last April, foreseeing the danger, we raised our voices in the most solemn manner against this disruptive and immoral principle. We pointed out to our young men the conscientious difficulties in which it would involve them, and warned them against it. Disregard of the Divine Law, then laid down by the bishops, is the chief cause of all our present sorrows and calamities.

We now again authoritatively renew that teaching; and warn our Catholic people that they are conscientiously bound to abide by it, subject, of course, to an appeal to the Holy See.

No one is justified in rebelling against the legitimate government, whatever it is, set up by the nation, and acting within its rights. The opposite doctrine is false, contrary to Christian morals, and opposed to the constant teaching of the Church. 'Let every soul,' says St Paul, 'be subject to the higher powers' that is, to the legitimate authority of the state. From St Paul downwards, the Church has inculcated obedience to authority, as a divine duty as well as a social necessity; and has reprobated unauthorised rebellion as sinful in itself and destructive of social stability: as it manifestly is. For if one section of the community has that right, so have other sections the same right, until we end in general anarchy. No one can evade this teaching, in our present case, by asserting that the legitimate authority in Ireland just now is not the Dáil or Provisional Government. That government has been elected by the nation, and is supported by the vast majority of public opinion. There is no other government, and cannot be, outside the body of the people. A Republic without popular recognition behind it is a contradiction in terms.

Such being the Divine Law, the guerrilla warfare now being carried on by the Irregulars is without moral sanction: and therefore the killing of National soldiers in the course of it is murder before God; the seizing of public or private property is robbery; the breaking of roads, bridges, and railways, is criminal destruction; the invasion of homes and the molestation of citizens a grievous crime.

All those who, in contravention of this teaching, participate in such crimes, are guilty of the gravest sins, and may not be absolved in Confession, nor admitted to Holy Communion, if they purpose to persevere in such evil courses.

It is said that there are some priests who approve of this Irregular insurrection. If there be any such, they are false to their sacred office, and are guilty of the gravest scandal, and will not be allowed to retain the faculties they hold from us. Furthermore we, each for his own diocese, hereby forbid under pain of suspension, *ipso facto*, reserved to the ordinary, any priest to advocate or encourage this revolt, publicly or privately.

Our people will observe that in all this there is no question of mere politics, but of what is morally right or wrong according to the Divine Law, in certain principles, and in a certain series of acts, whether carried out for political purposes or otherwise. What we condemn is the armed campaign now being carried on against the government set up by the nation. If any section in the community have a grievance, or disapprove of the national government, they have the elections to fall back upon, and such constitutional action as is recognised by God and civilised society. If their political views are founded on wisdom they will succeed sooner or later; but, one thing is certain, the Hand of Providence will not be forced, nor their cause advanced, by irreligion and crime.

It may perhaps be said that in this our teaching we wound the strong feelings of many of our people. That we know, and the thought is an agony to us. But we must teach the truth in this grave crisis, no matter what the consequences. It is not for want of sympathy with any part of our flock that we interfere, but from a deep and painful sense of our duty to God, to our people, and out of true charity to the young men themselves specially concerned. Let it not be said that this our teaching is due to political bias, and a desire to help one political party. If that were true, we were unworthy of our sacred office. Our religion, in such a supposition, were a mockery and a sham. We issue this Pastoral Letter under the gravest sense of our responsibility, mindful of the charge laid upon us by our Divine Father, to preach His doctrine, and safeguard His sacred rule of faith and morals, at any cost. We must, in the words of St Peter, 'Obey God rather than men'.

With all earnestness we appeal to the leaders of this saddest revolt to rise above their own feelings, to remember the claims of God, and the sufferings of the people, on their conscience; and to abandon methods which they now know, beyond the shadow of doubt, are un-Catholic and immoral, and look to the realisation of their ideals along lines sanctioned by Divine Law and the usages of well ordered society. Let them not think that we are insensible to their feelings. We think of them with compassion, carrying as they do on their shoulders the heavy responsibility for what is now happening in Ireland. Once more we beg and implore the young men of this movement, in the name of God, to return to their innocent homes, and make, if necessary, the big sacrifice of their own feelings for the common good. And surely it is no humiliation, having done their best, to abide by the verdict of Ireland.

We know that some of them are troubled and held back by the oath they took. A lawful oath is indeed a sacred bond between God and man; but no oath can bind any man to carry on a warfare against his own country, in circumstances forbidden by the law of God. It would be an offence to God and to the very nature of an oath to say so.

We therefore, hope and pray that they will take advantage of the government's present offer and make peace with their own country; a peace which will bring both happiness and honour to themselves, and joy to Ireland generally, and to the friends of Ireland all over the world.

In this lamentable upheaval, the moral sense of the people has, we fear, been badly shaken. We read with horror of the many murders recorded in the press. With feelings of shame we observe, that when country houses and public buildings were destroyed, the furniture and other fittings were seized and carried away by people in the neighbourhood. We remind them that all such property belongs in justice to the original owners, and now must be preserved for and restored to them by those who hold it.

We desire to impress on the people the duty of supporting the National Government, whatever it is; to set their faces resolutely against disorder; to pay their taxes, rents and annuities; and to assist the government, in every possible way, to restore order and establish peace. Unless they learn to do so, they can have no government; and, if they have no government, they can have no nation.

As human effort is fruitless without God's blessing, we exhort our priests and people to continue the prayers already ordered, and we direct that the remaining October devotions be offered up for peace. We also direct that a Novena to the Irish Saints, for the same end, be said in all public churches and oratories, and in semi-public oratories, to begin on the 28th of October and end on November the 5th, in preparation for the Feast of all the Irish Saints. These Novena devotions, in addition to the Rosary and Benediction, may include a special prayer for Ireland and the Litany of the Irish Saints.

THE SITUATION WAS ABOUT to change dramatically in the Tuam area, with the arrival of the first group of garda síochána in the town on 4 November 1922.

1   The Army must always be referred to as the 'Irish Army', the 'National Army', 'National Troops' or simply 'troops'.

2   The Irregulars must not be referred to as the 'Executive Forces' nor described as 'forces' or 'troops'.

3   Irregular leaders are not to be referred to as of any rank, such as 'Commandant' etc., or are not to be called officers.

4   Articles or letters as to the treatment of the 'irregular' prisoners may not be published.

5   The Censors are not to insert words of their own in any article submitted to them. Their business is to cancel what is objected to. They may however propose to substitute words or phrases such as 'Irregulars' for 'Republicans', 'fired at' for 'attacked', 'seized' for 'commandeered', 'kidnapped' for 'arrested'.

EXECUTIONS BEGIN
NOVEMBER – DECEMBER 1922

THE MONTH OF NOVEMBER 1922 marked the initiation by the Provisional pro-Treaty Government of a policy of 'official executions' of prisoners, several weeks before the Irish Free State came into being on 6 December 1922.

While, in theory, the constitution of the new Irish Free State, was supposed to be liberal, and provided for due process and the rule of law, the reality in December 1922, was quite different. Within 48 hours of the foundation of the new state, on 6 December 1922, the cabinet of William T. Cosgrave, now termed the Executive Council of the Irish Free State, descended to a new low, by executing prisoners of war, who had been held for many months without trial, and on cabinet diktat. This stained the reputation of all those connected with the process, and indeed the name of Ireland around the world.

One of the four men executed in Mountjoy Jail on the morning of 8 December 1922, was Liam Mellows whose statue stands today in Eyre Square in Galway. Mellows was not a native of Galway even though he had been active in Republican politics in the county ever since he led the biggest mobilisation in Ireland outside Dublin at Easter 1916.

Unlike De Valera in Clare, Mellows lost his standing as a TD in Co. Galway in the June 1922 general election, just as Erskine Childers lost his seat in Wicklow/Kildare. It is said the main reason why Mellows failed to be returned in Galway in 1922 was that he insisted in using the less familiar Irish version of his name, Liam Ó Maoilíosa, and it is alleged, huge numbers of voters failed to recognise it, even though they were native Irish speakers in many cases. It is interesting to note that the two Republican TDs who lost their seats, Childers and Mellows, were shot within a few months. Contrast this with General Tom Maguire, of the Second Western Division of the IRA, who was sentenced to death in Athlone in January 1923, along with five others because of their open war against the Free State. Maguire who was a TD for South Mayo and South Roscommon was not shot when the others were, probably because the Free State propaganda machine liked to perpetuate the myth that they did not shoot elected representatives – in spite of what happened to Cathal Brugha and Harry Boland in the summer of 1922.

Another popular Free State propaganda line was that the Cosgrave government selected one man from each province for execution on 8 December 1922 so that the message would go out to all parts of the country. Liam Mellows is supposed to have been the Connacht representative, even though he was born in England of Irish parents (farm labourers from South Leinster) and is buried near Gorey in Co. Wexford. Other factors influenced the rather arbitrary decision as to whom to shoot and not to shoot in government circles in those days; and as the chief government 'spin doctor' at the time, Desmond Fitzgerald is said to have burned the state files when Cumann na nGaedheal lost office in 1932, we shall never know the full story.

IRA LETTER OF WARNING, 1922

The following letter, signed Chief-of-Staff (for Army Council), was addressed to 'the Speaker of the Provisional Parliament of Southern Ireland', 27 November 1922

Sir,

The illegal body over which you preside has declared war on the soldiers of the Republic and suppressed the legitimate Parliament of the Irish Nation.

As your 'Parliament' and Army Headquarters well know, we on our side have at all times adhered to the recognised rules of warfare. In the early days of this war we took hundreds of your forces prisoners, but accorded to them all the rights of Prisoners-of-War and, over and above, treated them as fellow-countrymen and former comrades. Many of your soldiers have been released by us three times although captured with arms on each occasion. But the prisoners you have taken you have treated barbarously, and when helpless have tortured, wounded and murdered them.

We have definite proof that many of your senior officers including members of your 'Parliament' have been guilty of most brutal crimes towards the IRA prisoners and have reduced your soldiers to a state of savagery in some areas.

Finally you are now pretending to try IRA prisoners before your make-believe courts. You have already done to death five after such mock ceremonials. You now presume to murder and transport the soldiers who had brought Ireland victory when you, traitors, surrendered the Republic twelve months ago.

Next to the members of your 'Provisional Government' every member of your body who voted for this resolution by which you pretend to make legal the murder of soldiers is equally guilty. We therefore give you and each member of your body due notice that unless your army recognises the rules of warfare in the future we shall adopt very drastic measures to protect our forces.

Let us look at what J. J. Waldron had to say in his notes for those dark November and December days:

November 4th, 1922

The civic guards arrived in town last Friday and took possession of the old RIC barracks, now in a dilapidated condition. Certain elements in our midst not actually criminals, will be none the worse for the restraining influence of the policeman. The street brawler needs to be more careful, Saturday evening's pitch and toss school under the cross in the square will have to seek a more secluded venue and the all night pubs may be tempted to close a little earlier for their own sake if not for the customers. One member of the force was heartily welcomed. He was Sergeant Roddy. One can't forget his action in July 1920 when as a member of the RIC he refused to take part in the burning of the town. He then resigned [from] the force and was appointed craner by the commissioners, a position he held for a short time. He was visited one night at his residence and beaten up by masked men who threatened his life if he did not leave the town which he had to do for the sake of his family. Now he is back in charge of the new force.

November 11th, 1922

Some surprise mingled with indignation was evident in Tuam on

Tuesday, when four young men in the town were arrested by the Free State troops. The reason for arrest is unknown and puzzles the man in the street.

The arrested men are Michael Loftus, Bishop Street, William Hannon, Naughton's, Shop Street, P. Colleran, Walsh's, High Street, Jim and Tim McHugh, Hosty's, The Square; the latter house had to be closed temporarily owing to their arrest.

Soon after in Dáil Éireann a question was asked of General Mulcahy concerning their arrest. His answer was that Burke was believed to act as intelligence officer for the Republicans and Loftus as a carrier of dispatches, information which is held in grave doubt in the district.

November 18th, 1922

A search party of troops visited Headford last week in a round-up operation. About to search a house when a man was noticed running from the building, he was called on to halt and a Mauser rifle, four bombs and a quantity of ammunition was found in his possession. He gave his name as O'Brien and is believed to be from Tuam. On the way back to Galway the troops were ambushed on two occasions but failed to find the attackers and reached Galway without mishap.

November 22nd, 1922

Tuam again was the target for another raid by Republicans. At about 8 o'clock last night they marched casually through the town. Some proceeded to the workhouse and soon machine gun and rifle fire was opened on the building to which the garrison replied. When the attackers felt they had the troops rounded up, they started their usual *modus operandi* of commandeering supplies from several shops in town. The unusual commandeer on this occasion was four or five motor cars from local garages as well as two bicycles from the barracks. Others of the parties made an attempt to fire the signal cabin at the station but it refused to ignite. On their retreat, they cut down several trees of the plantation at the end of the Galway road to prevent pursuit. This was confession night for the First Friday and many people were caught in town from the Galway road area but their fears were allayed when Fathers Walsh, King and Moane accompanied them through the danger zone. It must be said in justice that the people in question were treated with great courtesy and helped over the obstacles.

The whole affair lasted over an hour and when the invaders left the whole town again settled to its wonted somnolence.

From the raid goods to the value of £29 was taken from Canny's of Bishop Street, £28 from O'Malley's of High Street, including some trench coats, two sides of bacon, value £7.18, from M.S. Walsh & Sons, High Street, Pat McHugh, The Square, Tobs.: Cigs, value £17, T. Waldron, High Street, goods £4-17-6.

December 8th, 1922

Army Proclamation published on this date from Portobello barracks, Dublin:

> That a conspiracy exists to assassinate the members of the nation's parliament. It has already claimed two victims.
>
> Any person found in possession of bombs, dynamite, gelignite or other explosive substance, revolver, rifle, gun, etc., or ammunition will be tried before any two members of the Army Council. In case the accused are found guilty such person will suffer death or other penalty prescribed.
>
> Signed: December 7th, 1922 on behalf of the Army Council, Risteard Ua Maolcatha, General Commander in Chief.

The two victims mentioned above were Pádraic Ó Máille and Seán Hales, both TDs, shot whilst travelling on a side car through Dublin. The former was wounded, the latter was killed.

Once their own lives were plainly in danger, the Leinster House deputies' support for the government's hardline measures began to waver. Mulcahy and Cosgrave had to move quickly to bring the dangerous new situation under control. One deputy who tried to resign was forced back by threats of treason charges. The government proved itself ruthless in ensuring its own survival.

Mulcahy went to Cosgrave's cabinet for consent to an official reprisal by which four leading Republican prisoners would be summarily executed without formality of trial, although held in prison since the surrender of the Four Courts, months before the special powers had been passed. There was no argument. The cabinet all gave their consent in turn. Eight men around the table agreed that the four should die to help guarantee their safety and the safety of the Free State.

In Mountjoy jail, early the next morning, on Sunday 8 December 1922, four men whose names live in Republican memory – Rory O'Connor, Liam Mellows, Joe McKelvey and Dick Barrett – were woken and told they would be shot at dawn.

PÁDRAIC Ó MÁILLE REPRESENTED THE single seat Connemara constituency in the first Dáil Éireann (1919–1921) and was one of the seven Sinn Féin TDs from the multi-seat Galway (city and county) constituency in the Second Dáil Éireann.

He retained his seat, as a pro-Treaty candidate in the June 1922 ('the Pact') election, the full result being as follows: Galway (seven seats); Electorate (81,455); Quota 4,563: [Figures on the right are First Preferences. The order of election is given on the left]

1. Patrick J. Hogan (pro-Treaty), 6,832
2. Pádraic Ó Máille (pro-Treaty), 6,445
3. Thomas J. O'Connell (Labour), 4,821
4. Joseph Whelehan (pro-Treaty), 4,361
5. George Nicolls (pro-Treaty), 2,258
6. Bryan Cusack (anti-Treaty), 4,425
7. Frank Fahy (anti-Treaty), 3,418

As I said already Liam Mellows (anti-Treaty) failed to be returned, even though he polled 3,937 first preferences, giving an overall

Galway result of four pro-Treaty and two anti-Treaty TDs plus one Labour deputy who was, in effect, also pro-Treaty. In the general election of August 1923, after the Civil War had been won by the Free State army, and the pro-Treaty deputies had established themselves in power as the Cumann na nGaedheal party, Ó Máille, who had been elected Leas-Cheann Comhairle, was returned again at No. 3 in what was now a nine-seater race under the new Free State electoral lay-out. This new arrangement also gave votes to women at the same age as men (21 or over) for the first time. Ó Máille came below Paddy Hogan and Herbert Charles Mellows, brother of Liam Mellows, who had been shot without trial by the government the previous 8 December 1922.

The following is a summary of the Galway result at the August 1923 election:

GALWAY (9 SEATS)

Electorate 106,093 – an increase of more than 25% from the previous year, because of the changes outlined above. The quota was 4,845.

1. Patrick J. Hogan (Cumann na nGaedheal) 7, 563
2. Herbert Charles Mellows (Sinn Féin Republican) 7,131
3. Pádraic Ó Máille (Cumann na nGaedheal) 6,570
4. Frank Fahy (Sinn Féin Republican) 5,670
5. George Nicolls (Cumann na nGaedheal) 1,732
6. Seán Broderick (Cumann na nGaedheal) 1,817
7. Louis E. O'Dea (Sinn Féin Republican) 1,413
8. Thomas J. O'Connell (Labour) 1,862
9. James Cosgrave (Independent) 1,922

This gave an overall result of: Cumann na nGaedheal 4, Sinn Féin Republican 3, Labour 1, Independent 1.

It was not very different from the result the year before, but given that some 10,000 Republicans were interned and many of their leading local activists had been shot in the Civil War, the swing against the Treaty seemed to become clear as soon as all women over 21 were given the vote, and the younger generation of men who had fought the British, but were not on the 1918 register, still in use in the summer of 1922, got access to the franchise.

The Cumann na nGaedheal back-benchers, who voted for the Treaty on the instructions of Collins and the IRB on the basis that it was a 'Stepping Stone' were realising that it was no such thing. Not only had they been forced to include an oath to the British monarch in the new constitution, but the deliberations of the Boundary Commission had still to come. In his inaugural speech as Head of the Free State government, W. T. Cosgrave emphasised what Derry City, Tyrone, Fermanagh, South Armagh and South Down had voted for, but never even hinted that these areas would be left not only under British rule, but under an even more unfair 'local majority' tyranny of the B-Specials, the Orange Order and the Stormont government.

When the issue came to a head, with the threat of an IRB coup in the army in 1924, Pádraic Ó Máille resigned his membership of Cumann na nGaedheal and formed part of the new protest group Clann Éireann. Other disillusioned pro-Treaty TDs, with IRB connections in many cases, resigned their seats altogether, in Carlow-Kilkenny, Cavan, Dublin North (two TDs) Dublin South, Sligo-Leitrim (two TDs), Mayo North and Roscommon. Ó Máille stood as a Clann Éireann candidate in the June 1927 general election, but lost his seat. He ran again in the September general election of that year as an Independent, but came last in a changed line-up now that De Valera's new party, Fianna Fáil, had subscribed to the oath and entered Leinster House. The September 1927 result in Galway saw Cumann na nGaedheal (Paddy Hogan, Seán Broderick, Martin McDonagh and Josie Mongan) elected, while there were five Fianna Fáilers (Frank Fahy, Seán Tubridy, Mark Killilea, Thomas Powell and Stephen Jordan). For the first time since the split about the Treaty five years earlier, there was a clear democratic majority in Galway against what had been pushed through with such reluctance and disregard for democracy, not to mention the bloody Civil War legacies. Three months previously, in the June 1927 general election, the issue was much less clear-cut with Cumann na nGaedheal (Hogan, Broderick, McDonagh), one National League (William John Duffy), one Labour (Gilbert Lynch) and four Fianna Fáil, still abstentionist, TDs (Killilea, Tubridy, Fahy and Powell) being returned. I understand that Pádraic Ó Máille joined Fianna Fáil later and was active in the party in the 1930s.

The tragic and complex nature of our freedom struggle is clear from the fact that it was the attack on Ó Máille and Seán Hales on 7 December 1922 (which was never claimed or sanctioned by the IRA) that was used as an excuse by the new Free State government to shoot Liam Mellows and other Republicans without trial. Yet, Ó Máille was to end up, over a decade later, supporting the Fianna Fáil party which grew out of the ruins of the Republicans' failure to win that Civil War.

Indeed in Galway the fact that the man whose memory is honoured in the Renmore military barracks, originally the headquarters of the British army Connaught Rangers regiment, Liam Ó Maoilíosa, was executed by the founding generation of that same 'National Army' is something which fascinates visitors from post-colonial countries around the world, when they visit Galway.

There are other entries for December 1922 in J. J. Waldron's notes as follows:

December 17th, 1922

Mr Martin Joe Nohilly, the popular master of the Tuam workhouse, was released from Galway Jail last Saturday after serving a sentence of nine months imprisonment by a military court for being alleged to have a gun in his possession whilst master of Tuam workhouse.

December 30th, 1922
Troops from Tuam and Ballinrobe operating in Headford area captured nine prisoners including T. O'Grady and Vincent Corcoran. The next day in the Shrule district at Caherlistrane they captured seven more when they surrounded Queally's public house.

BLOODLETTING EXTENDED
JANUARY 1923

BY CHRISTMAS 1922, THE Free State government had executed some 19 Republican prisoners under the Emergency Powers which gave decisions about life and death to the military council. Up to then all executions had taken place in Dublin but immediately after Christmas, as the Free State army tightened its grip in areas outside the capital, the toll began to mount in the provinces.

On 29 December 1922, two men, John Phelan and John Murphy, were shot in Kilkenny. The New Year executions began with five in Dublin on 8 January – Leo Dowling, Sylvester Heaney, Laurence Sheehy, Anthony O'Reilly and Terence Brady. Three others followed in Dundalk on 13 January – Thomas McKeown, John McNulty and Thomas Murray; four in Roscrea on 15 January – Francis Burke, Patrick Russell, Patrick MacNamara and Martin O'Shea – while James Lillis was sent to meet his maker in Carlow on the same date.

The toll of horror was spreading throughout the provinces, into almost every county and divisional area where the Free State army had triumphed. Every section of the army was being involved in blood and in bloody reprisals, not only in order to 'share the responsibility' but also to strike terror into each local area. A policy had been initiated of sentencing men to death, in a very arbitrary fashion, and then holding them without any date of execution, effectively as state hostages, in the hope that this would deter attacks on the new state forces as they moved into as yet unconquered areas. We shall see this again also in relation to the Tuam-Galway area.

The second half of January 1923 was more horrible than the first, as the policy of 'official executions' gained momentum, and the Free State army came under pressure to 'finish the war' before the longer summer days began, and before the tide of public opinion against what was being done in the name of a Free State Army Council began to change. The new phase began with four executions in Tralee – James Daly, John Clifford, Michael Brosnan and James Hanlon – and two in Limerick – Cornelius McMahon and Paddy Hennessy on 20 January 1923. General Mulcahy approved the execution of the four men in Tralee, the night before, by simply signing his signature on the back of a brown envelope. This was in response to a case for some 'deterrent' being necessary in Kerry, according to the local commander Pat O'Daly, who telegraphed Mulcahy for approval.

There were five other executions on that 20 January 1923 in Athlone, where the Western Command of the army was being entangled in the web. They are of particular interest to us because all five had Galway or western connections, as indeed had the sixth person, General Tom Maguire, TD who was also sentenced to death. As I have already said, the sentence was not carried out in Maguire's case, I suspect, because of his status as a TD. The five to die in Athlone were Thomas Hughes, Michael Walsh, Hubert Collins, Stephen Joyce and Martin Burke. Two days later, James Melia, Thomas Lennon and Joseph Ferguson were shot in Dundalk, while on 25 January Michael Fitzgerald and Patrick O'Reilly were executed in Waterford. On 26 January, Patrick Cunningham, William Conroy and Colm Kelly were shot in Birr, while on 27 January Patrick Geraghty and Joseph Byrne died in Port Laoise at the hands of former comrades.

J. J. Waldron's notes for 1923, from the Tuam area, need to be read in the context of this background. His entry for 27 January 1923 about the executions the previous week, is obviously mistaken when he suggests that four Headford men were executed in Limerick rather than Athlone. It is indicative of the confusion as well as the emotion generated at the time of writing, compounded

Standard letter sent to relatives of executed prisoners during the Civil War by the Free State authorities

no doubt, by the innocent, sad, almost pathetic letters written by some of the men to their relatives. But Mr Waldron begins his 1923 diary with an entry dated **January 13th, 1923:**

On Thursday night last Castle Hackett House was burned down. It was one of the finest mansions around Tuam. It contained many historic articles owned by the Kirwan family, now gone up in smoke and irreplaceable.

They had a very fine library with volumes going back 200 years. Perhaps the most precious loss felt by the family was the head of their famous racehorse 'The Friar' who saved the family estates, on whom they were bet, by winning the race.

It is estimated that the total loss will be in the region of £60,000, a remarkably high figure for the period. That happened on Thursday night last at ten o'clock when armed men surrounded the house and called on the caretaker to open the door. His wife who answered the call was told to clear out and take refuge in the steward's house. They were allowed time to remove their clothes and furniture. The reason they gave for the burning was that they expected the Free State army was going to occupy it.

They also said that they had no ill feelings against Col Bernard, the present owner, as he was a good man to the people in the locality.

January 16th, 1923

Free State troops searched the villages of Cloonfush, Barnaderg, Cloonthue, Lisavally, and cleaned the roads of obstruction. In Barnaderg in one house they seized a pile of drapery goods including blankets, books, knitting thread, men's suit lengths, and 8.5 doz. of handkerchiefs, etc., but nobody was arrested.

During the week things were very intense during the hours of darkness in the town of Tuam. The army had set up many fortified positions throughout the town against the Republicans. Many of the positions were attacked but the military were unable to locate the attackers.

After all the disturbances during the night the only casualty was a bullet hole through Naughton's Drapery Shop on Shop Street.

Some time later a column of Free State troops were refreshing themselves in Mrs O'Donnell's premises in Milltown after a long march when suddenly a crowd of men arrived with revolvers cocked, entered unobserved and held up the soldiers and disarmed them. They gathered both their small and large arms including a Lewis gun. (See introduction, p. 9–10)

January 27th, 1923

Executions

Eleven men were executed on Saturday last – five in Athlone – four in Tralee and two in Limerick and three on Monday in Dundalk.

They were found guilty of being in possession of arms and were implicated in attacks on the railway and other offences.

In Limerick *[this should read Athlone]* four of the men executed were from the Headford district and named as follows: Michael Walsh, Derrymore, Caherlistrane; Hubert Collins, Kickeen, Headford; Stephen Joyce, Derrymore, Caherlistrane and Martin Burke, Caherlistrane.

The Letters

Below are some of the letters of some of the men executed in Custume barracks Athlone on Saturday, 20 January 1923. Two men also executed in Tuam military barracks on 30 May, 1923. They also left a letter to be published of which I have a copy. I have a hazy recollection of the execution and I think those men were not natives in the Tuam area. *[The letter concerning 30 May 1923 is not included in Waldron notes. Nor does the Republican Roll of Honour recognise these two among the '77' on the Civil War list. Given the trauma of the situation it is easy to see how the early hours of Saturday 20 January are sometimes described as 'Friday night', and also the different spelling of 'Walshe' in the first letter.]*

Custume barracks,
Athlone,
Friday Night, January 20th, 1923

To dear Jim

Just a few lines before I pass away from this world forever. I suppose my time has come, so don't cry for my sake, life is sweet but we are getting a good chance of preparing for tomorrow.

Poor Tom Hughes is by my side, a soldier to the last. Stephen Joyce, Mick Walshe and Collins are going before God in the morning. I think with God's help I'm prepared to die, I don't know where this will find you but I will direct it to Ballinapark, the spot I loved best.

Poor old Dad, this will give him a blow, but it's a chance for a happy death. So goodbye until we meet in that happy land beyond the skies.

Goodbye from your loving brother,
Martin J. Burke

Custume barracks,
Athlone,
Friday Night, January 20th, 1923

Dear Kathleen,
I suppose you heard my fate before this reaches you. I would not die without writing to Ballinapark the spot I love best. But I bid goodbye for the last time on New Year's Eve. But goodbye Aunt Delia, Nora, May, Uncle Jack and poor Patrick. I am happy for we got a fair chance; we had the priest and will hear Mass in the morning. I'll see you reading this. I'll be singing with the angels when you are reading this. I am enclosing my beads as a keepsake. I am happy as I write this, I hope ye will remember me in your prayers. Remember me as the wild boy of the family.

Goodbye All,
From your dying cousin,
M. J. Burke

Custume barracks,
Athlone,
Friday Night, January 20th, 1923

Dear Patie,
I suppose by the time this reaches you my fate will be known. Well, Patie, don't cry or grieve for my sake, for it is God's will. My time in this world is at an end. Some time this day will come for us all. Mine is a happy one, I hope. So cheer up. Please God I will be looking down at you reading this. Poor old dad, will this kill him. Tell him I will soon be meeting him again. Pray for the repose of our souls.

Goodbye,
From your fond brother,
(Capt.) Martin J. Burke.

Custume barracks,
Athlone,
January 20th, 1923

Dear sister Julia
Just a few lines bidding you the last farewell. On tomorrow morning myself, M. Walsh, M. Burke, H. Collins and Thomas Hughes will meet our death at the hands of Irishmen, still we are quite happy and contented, we have been to see

a priest, we will hear them in the morning and receive the body and blood of our saviour tomorrow morning at 8 a.m. It will be the happiest hour of my life. I know this will come as a terrible shock to you. I fear your heart will break, I ask you not to grieve for me for it must be God's holy will that I should sacrifice my life for Ireland. It had been the dreams of my earliest youth, the music of the rifles have always been ringing in my ears since the day Cmdt Louis Darcy handed me his revolver and said hold this. Rather than part [with] it lose your life first. This I was determined to do as you know the consequences now. Tell mother and father not to grieve for me for all I ask now is to pray for me. I would not like to hear ye crying when I am amongst the dead, tell all my companions to pray for me Julia. I ask you to wear these medals in memory of your dead brother. God bless and protect you from all danger, goodbye now until I meet you in Heaven.

– From your loving brother, Stephen [Joyce].

Garrison Detention,
Custume Barracks,
Athlone, 19 January 1923

My Dearest Mother,
I again write you a few lines, but oh, Mother it is going to be the last. The last word to you on this side of the grave, as I am going to meet my great God tomorrow morning. But Mother Dear don't grieve for me as I am prepared to meet him who created me, to his likeness. But Dear Mother I know it shall grieve you all, but I ask one request of you not to worry but to pray for me because one prayer goes longer for me than all the sad tears that a nation could shed.

I am fully prepared for what poor Thomas wasn't.* Just yesterday two years he was put before the firing squad. And I hope to be with him by the time you get this letter. Oh, how happy he shall be to see me.

Dearest Mother I am sending you my Rosary beads. The beads I got from Father Kearney the day of Thomas' funeral. I can't stop but think how happy he shall be when he sees me and knows that I have died for the same ideal that he died for.

Dear Mother I now finish by sending you dear Mother my best love and also to Cissie, James and Joe. I shall write to them also.

So cheer up now we shall meet again in that happy land where there is no pain. Again I ask you all not to worry over this.

Goodbye and God bless you,
From your loving son,
Hubert [Collins].

* His brother, shot by the British in Headford on 22 January 1921 during the War of Independence. If the date (from the Galway Roll of Honour) is correct then the second anniversary was still three days away – and not 'two years ago yesterday'.

Garrison Detention,
Custume Barracks,
Athlone.

My Dear Joe,
As I drop you these few lines it is drawing nearer to my death. As I am about to die for loving my country they say, but I am proud of it. It is just one short month since I saw you all, how happy we were then. But I am as happy now, thanks be to the Great God, and in a few short hours I shall be with Him who made us all happy.

How happy I shall be when I meet our loving brother Thomas who died for the same thing just this week two years. But Joe, this world has no earthly charms for me now as I am ready to meet my God. But Joe I ask one request of you, I shall be sending a penknife home it belongs to Miss Rainey I took [it] from her, and also the flash lamp, Jim Lee has it at his house. Dear Joe I conclude by sending you, James and Mama, Cissie, my best love and God Bless you.

You need not worry about me as we shall all have to go and you might never get a chance of preparing for death like I have, so goodbye for now Joe.

Your Loving Brother,
Hubert [Collins].

Joe do help Mama and make her as happy as you can.

Goodbye, cheer up.
H.C.

Garrison Det.,
Custume Barracks,
Athlone, January 19, 1923

Dearest Bro. James,
Just a line from this side of the grave. A line to let you know that it is going to be the last ever again. For it now being about nine o'clock on Friday night and I shall stand before the firing squad at eight o'clock tomorrow Saturday morning.

Dear James don't worry about me as I am very happy and resigned to the will of God. The priest is going to be with us to the last.

We are all happy going to meet our God. We shall be happier in the next life. We have all got to die and we are getting a great chance of preparing ourselves to meet our loving Jesus.

So James try and cheer up Mama. I know that it shall be another great blow to her, but for God's sake try and console her – do James for me.

James dear, I am leaving you my overcoat, if they send it to you, and I also leave you my collar pin and tie clip (your own). God bless you all James dear I must finish now and hope you are as happy as I am. I send you, Mama, Joe and Cissie my very best love.

Goodbye, cheer up and have courage.
From your loving brother,
Hubert [Collins].

Custume Barracks,
Athlone, Jan. 19, 1923

Cissie Dear,
It is hard for me to find words to say to you, but all I say now will be the last for me on this earth, but I shall be before you all in the next to meet you.

Cissie dear, you that used to write to me the nice letters, if I only knew the last time I was talking to you that it would be the last to see you on this earth, how I would hug and kiss you, you that was so nice to me always, but Dearest Cissie all I can leave you is the handkerchief you sent me and also leave you all my little scissors, I think it was Jim Lee that gave it to me, I will write to him also.

Cissie dearest, don't grieve or worry after me, pray for me and I will pray for you, think of what I die for, that is great and glorious for one to die for one's country. Cissie it is grand to be going to meet a King, a King of kings. I am well prepared now as the priest is only after leaving us and we are going to Mass on tomorrow morning and receive the Blessed Sacrament and then to be off with our Blessed Lord.

Stephen Joyce, Martin Burke and Tommy Hughes are coming with me. We shall all meet you when you come to us.

Cissie dear, I must now come to a finish both in this note and in this life, so goodbye, cheer up Cissie dear. I am sending you all my very best love.

From your loving brother
Hubert [Collins].

P.S. Cissie dear, cheer up Mama, tell her that she don't know how happy I am, tell her not to shed one tear for me, but pray.

H. Collins

Remember me Cissie to all my neighbours, to Aunt Kit, Tommy McDonagh, wife and father also to Dan Finn.

H.C.

The following is taken from the local Athlone paper The Westmeath Independent *dated 27 January 1923:*

As already announced one of the five young men executed at Custume Barracks, Athlone, on last Saturday morning was Mr Thomas Hughes, eldest son of Mr Patrick and Mrs Hughes of Boginfin, Athlone. He was aged 21 years and received his education at St Peter's Convent and subsequently at the Marist Brothers' Schools, Athlone. During the Black and Tan terror he was armoury officer of the local IRA Brigade, a position which he held up to the time of the division in the ranks, having been present at the taking over of the Custume Barracks from the British.

He had been 'on the run' for seven months and was captured by the National troops on December 20th last and it was not until 6 p.m. on the day of his execution that his afflicted parents were officially notified of the event. On being blindfolded he shook hands with some of his captors requesting them to inform his mother that his last thoughts were of her.

Solemn Requiem Mass was celebrated in St Peter's church on Tuesday last for the repose of the soul of the deceased before a large congregation. Rev. Fr O'Reilly, CC, was celebrant; Rev. Fr Neary, CC, deacon; Rev. Fr Fallon, CC, sub-deacon; The Very Rev. Canon Crowe, PP, and Rev. Fr Gilooly, CC, were in the choir and the chief mourners were: – Patrick Hughes (father), Mrs Hughes (mother), Mrs Monaghan (grandmother), Dotie, Pearl, Maud, Eileen and Josie (sisters), Jim (brother), Mrs Hardiman, Mrs Quinn and Miss Monaghan (aunts).

His last letters:
We have been requested to publish the following letters written by the late Mr Thomas Hughes to his relatives prior to his execution:

My Darling Mother,
It is now 6 p.m. We are just after being told that we are to be executed in the morning at 8 o'clock. Do not fret for me, as with God's Holy Will, I will be prepared to meet Him, as it is a grand thing to get timely warning before you die. I hope I will be in Heaven before you receive this sad greeting. Well, welcome be the Will of God. Remember mother, if it is the Will of God that He receives me, I will be always watching over yourself, Dad, Dotie, Pearl, Maud, Eileen, Jim and Josie. Try and bear up mother and please God we will all be together again in the time to come. I am writing to grandma and some of my friends. My companions and I do not bear any malice against those who are going to carry out the deed. Goodbye for the present.

Your Loving Son,
Tom

P.S. – You will get a crucifix and prayer book from some of the officers.

My Dearest Dad,
It is now 6.30 p.m. We were just now informed that four comrades, namely, Martin Burke, Michael Walsh, Hubert Collins and Stephen Joyce and myself are to be executed in the morning at 8 a.m. We are all to be attended by Canon Crowe and Father Columba tonight and have Mass in the morning. So we have plenty of time to prepare to meet our God. Dad, try and console poor mother and tell her that I am not afraid to die. 10.30 p.m. – We are just after getting Confession now from Father O'Reilly and had a very nice chat with him. He said he would call to see you. I am leaving my beads to you, dear Dad, and my crucifix to mother.

Your Loving Son,
Tom

My Dear Sister Pearl,
Just a line to let you know I am about to be executed in the morning. Pearl, do not fret for me. Try and console poor mother and Dad, because I know it will be a terrible blow to them. I feel very happy tonight and am prepared to

die. It is not everyone who has 12 hours for same. Do not forget to write to some of the lads here as they long for a letter from outside. Well, goodbye and God Bless you.

Your Affectionate Brother,
Tom

My Dear Sister Dotie,

Just a line bidding you my last farewell on this earth. But, Dotie, keep your heart up and do not fret for me as with God's help I will be happy. I am sending you a small pocket looking-glass for a souvenir. Try and cheer up mother as I know this will be a terrible blow to her. Bid goodbye for me to all my friends.

Your Affectionate Brother,
Tom

My Dear Grandma,

Sorry to say this is the last time you will get a letter from me, as myself and four comrades are going to meet our God in the morning. Grandma, don't fret for me. I will meet the firing squad just like a soldier should. I am feeling happy now since I had Confession. We will receive Holy Communion at 7 a.m. in the morning. We were attended by Father O'Reilly as Canon Crowe is away. I know it will be a terrible blow to you and poor Mother, but all you can do is say a prayer for my comrades and myself.

The Free State officers and men are as nice as they can be to us and you must not think I am dying bearing any malice towards them. I forgave them as they are only doing what they think is their duty. I only hope I will be with Grandma and Kit before you receive this note. And again, cheer up, Grandma, and say 'it is no crime to die in a noble cause'. Bid my last goodbye to Katie, Pearl, Pat, Lil and family, Tiny and family, Dick and family, Joe and family, and all in the house. Well, dear Grandma, I think I have enough said now. Goodbye and God Bless you all.

Your Affectionate Grandson,
Tom.

P.S. – I will have a crucifix for you if I can. Don't forget to pray for me.

Tom.

LULL AND BARBARITY IN HOSTILITIES
FEBRUARY—APRIL 1923

FOLLOWING THE HORRIBLE BLOOD-LETTING at official level in January 1923 there seems to have been a lull in the course of the Civil War hostilities during February.

Already the toll of 'official executions' had reached 55 in the three winter months of November, December and January. During the month of February 1923 there was only one Free State execution when Thomas Gibson, a former Free State soldier, faced the firing squad in Portlaoise. This is why the shootings of the 21 Republicans – including the six at Tuam – in the months of March, April and May 1923 (even after the ceasefire had come into effect by the IRA on 30 April) left such a bitter taste.

But hostilities, raids and round-ups continued in the Tuam area during February and into March 1923. J. J. Waldron deals in particular with the raid on Cluid and the capture of 18 Republican prisoners at the end of that episode on 19 February 1923. Most of these prisoners were sentenced to death, shortly afterwards, and held as hostages in Galway and Tuam against the 'good behaviour' of other local IRA groups.

It was from these prisoners of war that the six men were selected for execution in Tuam on 11 April 1923, following an IRA attack on Headford on 9 April 1923. The policy of state hostage-taking was still in use as those arrested in Cluid could not possibly have had anything to do with the Headford attack. But they had been sentenced to death, and then held as hostages, for execution on an arbitrary basis as soon as some other incident annoyed the Free State leaders. The Waldron notes for February 1923 begin as follows:

February 3rd, 1923

On Saturday last a young man named Geddes was arrested in his father's house, Bishop Street, Tuam and brought to the military barracks.

The Free State army took over possession of the Hibernian Hall in Vicar Street last week and erected a sandbagged shelter outside on the path. The situation controls the Mall and the railway station and is near the guards' barracks. Military patrols also parade the town at night. This is relied on as a method of defence and protection for the men in case of further raids.

Mr Michael Loftus, Jnr, who had been detained in Athlone barracks was released on Friday last.

February 10th, 1923

The military operating from Claremorris made some important captures in Milltown, Co. Galway during the weekend. They first of all surrounded a farmhouse and took three prisoners and then went in the direction of Dunmore. They returned to Milltown by another route and surprised a party of men engaged in demolishing the local barracks and arrested them.

The names of the prisoners are not given; they are alleged to have taken a gun (Lewis) about six weeks ago.

The following escaped from military custody in Claremorris; John and Dan McCormack, Liskeavy and Peter Burke, Knock, Milltown.

The Raid at Cluid

At 3 a.m. one morning during the week of February 19th, 1923 Capt. MacElligott set off from Galway barracks with thirty men under his charge. They were skirmishing in the fields near Cluid at 6 a.m. whilst the country was still in darkness intensified with cold showers of sleet. The howling of the storm prevented any sound of their movements being heard. The troops moved with caution and noticed about

200 yards from them, some shadowed figures moving around a group of four houses.

Having encircled the buildings and men before the latter were aware of what was happening, Captain MacElligott then delivered a loud challenge.

Immediately there was a dash for cover in the houses and the bright flashes of fire from the army rifles. One section of the men took refuge in an old barn so Captain MacElligott called on them to come forth but there was no answer to the challenge.

There was a bomb then thrown on the roof of the barn and the troops awaited further developments.

After a short time, the eight men inside saw that there was no other alternative, as they were surrounded by superior forces, but to surrender.

They appeared at the small door of the barn with a white flag, hands raised above their heads, all wearing new trench coats.

Their leader admitted that they were completely taken by surprise, never expecting to be disturbed at such an early hour.

The cordon then gradually drew closer to the farm houses, when it was noticed that one man was trying to escape making a furious dash to get through the lines.

The captain called on him to halt and fired a shot over his head but he continued to run notwithstanding. Another shot was fired direct at him and he was seen to fall, mortally wounded. The remaining ten then surrendered and were thereupon marched into Galway, a distance of 15 miles where they arrived about three o'clock in the afternoon. The equipment captured included 15 Lee Enfield rifles, three Mauser rifles, a large land mine, a number of bombs, revolvers, new trench coats and leggings and Sam Brown belts.

All the arms were well oiled and in excellent condition. The men had been billeting in the small group of houses overnight.

The following are the prisoners captured at Cluid: *John Newell,

Headford; Pat Farragher, Kilmaine, Co. Mayo; Michael Joyce, Headford; James Craddock, Headford; *Martin Moylan, Farmerstown, Annaghdown; Patrick Jennings, Milltown; Thomas Madden, Caherlistrane; Edward Dooley, Headford; Michael Sweeney, Seefin, Claremorris; Batty Canavan, Mossfort; John Hession, Turlane, Caherlistrane; Michael Connolly, Hollymount, Co. Mayo; *Michael Monaghan, Headford; *Francis Cunnane, Headford; *†John Maguire, Cross, Cong; Joseph Collins, Kilkeel, Headford; Peter Brennan, Milltown, and *Séamus O'Malley, Oughterard.

The following report was issued from army headquarters, Portobello barracks, the day after the engagement. 'Troops operating in North Galway captured a column of Republicans, 18-strong, all of whom were fully armed. A short engagement preceded the capture, in the course of which one Republican was mortally wounded'.

THE MONTH OF MARCH 1923 got off to a very bad start and 22 people were killed within a few short days. In Ballyseedy, eight of the nine men selected for death were blown to bits; at Countess Bridge near Killarney, four IRA prisoners died on the same day, and at Bahaghs, Cahirciveen, five more men were shot and then put on a mine and blown to pieces on 12 March. On 13 March three were executed in Wexford – James Pearle, Patrick Hogan and John Creane – as well as James O'Rourke in Dublin, and William Healy in Cork.

Then, on the following day, the Free State policy of executing their prisoners extended beyond Leinster and Munster into Ulster when Charlie Daly, Tim O'Sullivan, Dan Enright and Seán Larkin were executed at Drumboe Castle, Co. Donegal. The shootings in the north-west were a cause of particular outrage, because three of these IRA men, Daly, O'Sullivan and Enright, had been sent northwards from their native Kerry to boost resistance at a time when even some of the pro-Treaty cabinet agreed that Collins' policy of

*These six men were the people executed in Tuam almost two months later on 11 April 1923.
†Younger brother of Commdt Tom Maguire, TD, Second Western Division. The surname is sometimes spelt McGuire, especially in formal Free State documents.

assisting the IRA in the north was the right one. The fourth IRA man shot in Drumboe, Seán Larkin, was from Co. Derry.

With the symbolic spilling of Kerry and Derry blood on what was later to become the border between Donegal and Tyrone, the Free State army toll of 'official executions' had come to 65, before St Patrick's Day 1923. The next horrific increase to 71 would see the extension of the shooting of prisoners, effectively being held as hostages, into Connacht, in Tuam workhouse, on 11 April 1923.

The only other entry in the Waldron notes for the month of March, from the Tuam area, concerns 3 March 1923: 'in the round up from Tuam barracks, the following were arrested: Joe Donnellan, Ryehill; Thomas Concannon, Lavally; John Newell, Belclare; Wm. Fahy, Feigh, Ballyglunin; Mal. Higgins, Ballyglunin; M. McDonagh, Barna; Michael Leonard, Belclare; Matt and Michael Garvey, Sylane, Tuam; Peter Canney, Belclare; Thomas Connolly, Russeltown, Milltown; James Hynes, Barnaderg and James Burke, Ryehill.

'In all about 200 prisoners, detained in Tuam barracks were removed last week (probably to Athlone).'

PEACE MOVES IN APRIL 1923 ...

BY APRIL 1923, ACCORDING to Dorothy Macardle 'it had become known to the Free State government that nearly all the leaders of the Republican Army were somewhere among the mountains of Tipperary and Waterford, and thousands of troops were concentrated on an encircling movement there'. IRA Chief-of-Staff Liam Lynch contended that the Western Division of the IRA was less hard-pressed than the Southern Division and that through these, the situation might yet be retrieved. But Seán Hyde, who was in command in the west, was not able to attend the March IRA convention in South Tipperary, nor was P. J. Ruttledge, vice-president of the Republic, mandated to stand in for De Valera as necessary.

Plans were afoot for the purchase of mountain cannons from Germany and this, it was felt, would enable the guerrilla columns still entrenched in their own areas to continue, if not indefinitely, at least until the following autumn and winter. Dev had reported for duty as an ordinary volunteer during the Civil War, and though recognised universally as President of Sinn Féin and the Irish Republic, held the military rank of adjutant to Seán Moylan, Cork No. 4 Brigade. Dev was instructed to take necessary steps to draw up terms for an honourable peace.

It was agreed that the Army Executive would meet again on 10 April 1923 when the Western delegates might be able to attend. But the early days of April were full of calamity for the Republican cause. The IRA Adjutant General, Tom Derrig, was captured in Dublin and wounded trying to escape. Then, on 10 April, on the slopes of the Knockmealdown Mountains, General Liam Lynch, on his way to the convention, was wounded in a skirmish with Free State troops at Crohan West, about three miles south-west of Newcastle. He died that night. The Free State soldier who shot Lynch at long distance as he descended those hills for cover is said to have shouted: 'We have got the Long Fellow'!

On the following day, 11 April 1923, came news of the six executions in Tuam.

Austin Stack, Kerry TD and member of the Republican cabinet, was captured on his way to the adjourned (again) meeting to discuss peace. A few days later, four more Republican commandants were captured. The adjourned meeting of the IRA executive finally met at Poulnacapple, near Mullinahone, Co. Tipperary on 20 April 1923. Frank Aiken, from the Fourth Northern Division, operating in the Louth-Armagh-South Down area, became Chief-of-Staff, and he and three other commandants, Liam Pilkington and Seán Hyde from the west, and Tom Barry from Cork were sent to Dublin as a Special Army Council to get De Valera, as President of Sinn Féin and the Republic, to announce the calling-off of hostilities. He issued a statement – having consulted the members of his Republican cabinet who were not in jail: P. J. Ruttledge, M. P. Colivet and Donal O'Callaghan – on 27 April 1923. The decision was taken by the IRA but announced by De Valera as President of Sinn Féin. A 'dump arms' order was prepared and the ceasefire came into operation on 30 April at mid-day.

Both Aiken and the IRA Council, as well as De Valera, outlined basic principles which they said were necessary if there was to be a 'political way forward' for the solution of the situation in which Ireland found itself at the end of the Civil War. These were:

1. The sovereignty of the Irish nation and the integrity of its territory are inalienable.
2. Any instrument purporting to the contrary is, to the extent of its violation of the above principle, null and void.

A rather stark and blunt declaration at a time when we again hear suggestions about what the Irish nation might be asked to sacrifice as part of the latest attempt to bring peace within the flawed partition structures, originally laid down in the 1920 British Government of Ireland Act.

I WILL LET THE WALDRON NOTES of the period speak for themselves:

April 3rd, 1923

This week there was a sensational escape from Galway Jail by fourteen prisoners. There is no information as to their identity but it is reported that some of them are men awaiting a sentence. Searching enquiries are being made by the authorities and disciplinary action is threatened to be taken against any persons who are found responsible. This could mean the authorities think this escape was an outside job.

Civic guards from Tuam in charge of Sergeant Roddy searched pubs in Headford on the 22nd Ult. and seized poteen found on the premises of Thady McHugh wrapped up in clothes in a box, one gallon of the liquid. There were also some small bottles of the stuff found in the house of Patrick Reilly.

Troops report that whilst operating between Headford and Galway they sent on ahead a motor with soldiers as [a] decoy. As they proceeded, suddenly the Republicans appeared [on] each side of the road and surrounded the motor. When the larger section of the troops put in appearance, the Republicans had to retreat, but not before fifteen were captured.

Attack on Headford on April 9th, 1923

A large scale attack by Republicans on the military post in Headford took place early in the morning of April 9th, 1923 and lasted nearly an hour.

It started at 1.15 a.m. when the Republicans came across the Corrib in boats from the Oughterard direction. They took up positions in Thady McHugh's public house which is opposite the barrack, formerly the National Bank, and also the house of the local minister nearby.

Two of the attackers in stockinged feet crossed the road and laid a mine on the wire entanglement in front of the barrack door.

When the bomb exploded it blew in the door and broke many windows in the area.

Shooting started from both sides immediately and the military gunner Sergt Carty brought his machine gun into action in the direction of McHugh's house. The first fatality was on the Republican side when a young man named McCormack was badly wounded, having a part of his leg and arm torn away by a bullet.

After some time the firing ceased and during the calm a shout was heard calling on the troops to come out and fight.

Captain Nugent who was in charge immediately stepped out onto the road followed by Lieut Burns and Gunner Carty with his machine gun.

They were not fully dressed as they were taken unawares and had not been long in bed.

Shooting started again and the first casualty was Sergt Carty who was hit by a bullet, and died later in Galway Hospital. After some time it was noticed that the Republican forces were gradually retreating towards the Corrib. Captain Nugent got his men to make a thorough search of the area and they came across numerous patches of blood on the ground; following the trail they found a dead body in a nearby yard. It was the body of a well-known Tuam Republican John Higgins who in pre-Treaty days took an active part against the British.

Directing that the body be brought to the barracks the captain continued the search through the demesne, meeting up with about sixteen of the Republicans who they attacked but the machine gun jammed in the hands of the assistant gunner who himself was wounded and died the next day. The Republicans got clear away with their wounded leaving behind five rifles, twenty bombs, a battery and seven large cable wires, some coats and boots – they were all evidently in their stockinged feet. It was stated that the Republicans intended planting a second mine but when the engineers were called they did not respond. No explanation was given. The mine was found afterwards by the troops.

Capt. Nugent's forces had five wounded and two deaths, the latter from wounds. He must be given credit as a brave man for defending his post. A Clareman, he was an experienced fighter in the old days, especially in the ambushes against the British ...

Both Dr Golding and Fr Daly gave all the comfort and assistance they could to the wounded.

The body of John Higgins was brought to the military barracks, Tuam and later handed over to his relatives and after Requiem High Mass in the cathedral was buried in the family plot in Kilbannon graveyard.

The injured Republican soldier was Lieut Daniel McCormack of Milltown.

Six Executions in Tuam

Sequel to the fight at Cluide* near Headford in February 1923: The following notice was issued on Wednesday morning from GHQ:

'James O'Malley, Oughterard;
Francis Cunnane, Kilcoona, Headford;
John Newell, Winefort, Headford;
John McGuire,* Cross, Cong;
Michael Monaghan, Clooneen, Headford;
Martin Moylan, Farmerstown, Annaghdown.

'All the above were charged with having possession of a rifle and ammunition at Cluide on February 21st, 1923 without proper authority.

'All six persons were found guilty. The findings were confirmed in each case and the prisoners were sentenced to death.

'The executions were duly carried out in Tuam military barracks (workhouse) on the morning of Wed., April 11th, 1923.'

THE MEN WERE EXECUTED IN parties of three and met their death bravely as Christians and were resigned to the will of God. For proof of that fact, read the last letters [below] from some of them written before their execution to relatives and friends.

They were attended during the night by two priests from the

*Usually spelt Cluid.
*Also spelt Maguire especially by his brother Tom

Tuam presbytery and in the morning they all attended early Mass at which two of them served.

The priests were with them to the last and as each fell they were given the last rites.

The bodies were interred in the garden nearby.

The report of the six executions carried out in Tuam sent a gloom over the town. So unexpected and tragic and indeed it can be said by one who was a resident of the town at the time that every single person felt the greatest sympathy for the families and relatives of the executed men.

One wonders why the executions were carried out in a small town like Tuam instead of some of the large centres? The answer may have been on account of the events in Headford, as several of the executed men were from that area.

Last letters

In the Reception Ward,
Galway Gaol, 1923

Dear Mother,

You are aware perhaps by now that I am one of the destined by God, to swell the roll of that martyred band who died for Ireland. I am going to my grave dying as I lived, believing that I did the best for my country and that the sacrifice will atone for anything left undone by me; that I have conscientiously done everything for the better interests of my country, according to my lights.

I have no dread, therefore it is with composure I accept my sentence, bearing no hatred against any living soul. To all my friends too numerous to mention, give them my best and sincerest love. For their many kindnesses during and after my intercourse with them, I am more than grateful and I trust that God will in some way repay them as I intended doing. But now that I am leaving them for a happier exchange, I am debarred from fulfilling my desire in this world of sorrows.

Well Mother, I know my death will shock you and all at home, but my dying wish is that no grief or sorrow be unnecessarily displayed by any of you for the end must come some time and is as welcome now as at any future date. And perhaps when I am no better prepared than now I hope God will accept my sacrifice for any faults I may have committed during my life on earth – my death is a glorious one, and I am unworthy of it.

There may be some who think our line of action a hopeless and foolish one, but the voices of Pearse and Plunkett and those who died for the same cause in 1916 inspired me to follow in their footsteps and I am confident the vindication of the sacred cause will come in some generation or another. Cheer up, Mother dear, I shall meet you in Heaven in the near future, though I hope your life on this earth shall be long and happy so much so that you will be recompensed in some small measure for your past and present worries.

Give to all my neighbours and companions of my childhood my dying wish for their future welfare, and to my loyal comrades a fond farewell. And let no act of vengeance mar the cause for which I die. Let that sanctified flag be borne aloft unstained by the son of Cain, so that the world will see we are not waging a war of Bolshevism of which the IRA are accused. I am sending you a few souvenirs including a pair of beads I got from Cissie during the Black and Tan regime. In them find consolation and do not worry.

Now I must conclude finally and eternally in this side of the grave so I send you Father, Cissie, Tessie, Bertie, Gerald, Willie, John, Tommie, Martin, Charles, Joe and Vincent my blessing and good wishes. May God bless all of you and may we all meet in Heaven, is the sincere wish of your dutiful and loving son.

Frank [Cunnane]

Tuam Barracks,
10/4/1923

My Dearest sister Tessie,
For the last time on this side of the grave I whisper my last farewell message to you. I ask you to cheer up and be brave. My body is lifeless but my spirit lives on. I am fully prepared to go to Him who made me. As I must die some time it is better that I should die now, since it is for Ireland I am to die.

To the Dooleys, Farraghers, Combers, Burkes, Manus Flynn, Nevells, Craddocks, give my last farewell, and tell them to say a prayer for me. Rem [ember] me to Cissie and tell her that in death I wear the scapulars she gave me. My Rosary Beads I send home. To the Mirehill, Crossursa and Horse Valley friends give my last love. Now Tessie dear, bear up, look on the bright side. I ask you all at home to be reconciled to God's will. Goodbye and may God bless you and guide you always in this world and on to the next. Cheerio with love, Your loving brother,

Frank [Cunnane]

Tuam Barracks,
10/4/1923

Dear Jim,
Tomorrow morning I am going to meet my God and join the goodly company of men who died for Ireland. We are after getting confession and I am very happy. Fr King and Fr Cunningham are here with us for the night so you can imagine how happy we are. Dear Jim it is not so hard as you think, it is worse for you and the poor people at home. Remember me to T. Joyce, J. Collins, M.

Sweeney, E. Dooley, T. Madden, M. Conneely, P. Farragher, M. O'Brien, Duignan and all our comrades in the other half of the Jail. Tell all to pray for us. Send a letter to my people at home, it will console them a little as you know it will be hard on them. Remember me also to Ray Colleran, Jim Lee, E. Conneely, G. Murphy and Petie Dooley and all my former comrades. We sang a few songs here tonight, M. Moylan, Jim O'Malley and myself so you can see we are not downhearted. Dear Jim I must conclude, goodbye forever and God bless you all. I hope we will be the last to die for Ireland. Goodbye once more.

From your fond companion,
Mickey Monaghan,
(Clooneen, Headford).

IRA Ceasefire
30 April 1923

THE EXECUTION OF SIX LOCAL men in the old workhouse in Tuam on 11 April 1923 was seen by many as an extension of the Army Council policy of Dick Mulcahy and Eoin O'Duffy of making certain that all fingers were steeped in bloody executions while the reign of arbitrary military terror existed; so that all the blame would not rest with the leaders later on. The politicians, with their very doubtful mandate for anything even half as drastic as the measures being taken to push through the Treaty, escaped with very little criticism at the time. In contrast, De Valera, head of the political Republicans, was blamed for every IRA action while the Cosgrave Free State government, which was, in theory, in charge of the National Army, and was supposed to be fighting for the principle of political control over the army, handed over the entire pursuit of the war, including the power of life or death of prisoners, to a military council.

It was as ironic, and sad, as those who argued that the Free State were 'fighting for democracy' included a compulsory oath of allegiance to a British crown. Critics of De Valera attack him for dismissing the oath requirement as an 'empty formula' after he founded Fianna Fáil and wanted to enter the Dáil. These same critics are less anxious to remind us of the fact that the original Irish Free State Constitution provided for the right of initiation by citizens in one of the liberal provisions of that document that had any relevance in the 1920s.

Article 48 of the Free State Constitution stated in part:

The Oireachtas may provide for the initiation by the people of proposals for laws or constitutional amendments. Should the Oireachtas fail to make such provisions, within two years, it shall, on the petition of not less than seventy-five thousand voters on the register, of whom, not more than fifteen thousand shall be voters in any one constituency, either make such provisions or submit the question to the people for decision, in accordance with the ordinary regulations governing the Referendum.

Proposals for having proposed bills passed by the Oireachtas submitted to the people in a referendum had been outlined in Article 47. But, Article 50 also provided that changes in the Constitution could be made by the majority in the two houses of the Oireachtas, Dáil and Seanad, by simple majority, and without a referendum, in the first eight years of the life of the new Free State. This is usually provided for in such circumstances, to tidy up obvious oversights or unworkable details as they emerge in practice in a new constitutional situation. When Éamon De Valera and his new Fianna Fáil party set about seeking a referendum on the crucial issue of the oath in 1926, and when it seemed likely not only that he could collect the 75,000 signatures but would probably win the referendum, the Cumann na nGaedheal government of Mr Cosgrave, in spite of its great claims for 'democracy', abolished the provision of the people's right on Initiation by simple legislation within the eight-year limit that had been laid down. Some people argued, at the time, that the eight-year period of free-hand to the government without having to consult the people was too long, given that the normal lifespan of a Dáil session was five years at a maximum. What is significant is that the Free State 'democrats' abolished the Right of Initiation and the people of the 26 counties have not had it restored to them ever since. De Valera, in his second coming as a 26-county democrat, did present Bunreacht na hÉireann to the people in 1937, but changes in that Constitution cannot be demanded by a group of concerned citizens. The initiative with regard to any referendum for change rests with the Dáil parties.

To GO BACK TO THE aftermath of the Tuam executions and the reaction in the town in April 1923 I quote from J. J. Waldron's notes:

At a meeting of the Tuam Town Commissioners held on 17 April 1923 the following resolution was proposed by Mr John Burke, TC [Editor of *The Tuam Herald*]:

'That we hereby record our disapproval of, and sorrow at, the executions carried out in this town on Wednesday morning last, and we equally condemn attacks on the National Forces, and reprisals, by whomsoever (committed) that we respectfully request his grace the Archbishop of Tuam and through him, the other bishops of Ireland to use their influence with the Free State government to have a stop put to such executions in future, as already enough blood has been spilled and young lives sacrificed in this unholy war.

'Further that we join with other public bodies in the suggestion that Monsignor Luzio the Papal Envoy be invited to act as intermediary between the two contending parties to negotiate an honourable peace, and thus bring to an end the horrible conditions now existing, which are a disgrace to the name of Ireland.

'That we tender to the bereaved parents and relatives of the deceased young men our heartfelt sympathy and we are of opinion that as Liam Lynch, one of the leaders, was accorded a public funeral this week, the bodies of the executed men should be given over to their relatives for interment. That copies of this resolution be sent to the Archbishop, the ministers of Dáil Éireann, and the TDs for this county.'

Mr Burke in proposing the resolution said the people of Tuam were shocked and pained at these terrible prosecutions. They heard a great deal nowadays of the old Gaelic civilisation and building up a Gaelic State. If the Gaelic State could only be built up by the execution of young Irishmen, he feared it would have a poor foundation. He was no supporter of Republican attacks on the people's government or violence in any shape or form.

In seconding the resolution Mr James Moran, TC, said it was a most painful duty for him as he knew most of the parents of the boys executed – parents who brought up their children as Catholics and patriotic as any were brought up in any place in Ireland.

Little he thought honest parents would meet with such a fate as seeing their children in the prime of life taken from them at the hands of their own countrymen. To the parents and sisters (one of whom is a nun in the Mercy Convent, Tuam) of the deceased they tendered their deepest sympathy to all.

The resolution was passed unanimously.

The following was sent to the Tuam Town Commissioners by Most Rev. Dr Gilmartin Archbishop of Tuam commenting on a resolution passed by them at a meeting on 17 April 1923.

> Dear Sir,
> In reply to your resolution, I have to say I have already expressed my sympathy with the people of Tuam in the horror we felt at the Tuam executions and the deaths which preceded them. I wish to join with your body in offering sympathy to the parents and relatives of all deceased. May all their souls rest in peace, Amen.
> As in the past I hope to use whatever influence I possess to put an end to all the violence and counter violence, as there is a constitutional way of composing our discords, existing conditions are a disgrace.
> I join with you in praying Mgr Luzio's mission may be crowned with success.
> Yours very faithfully,
> T. P. Gilmartin,
> Archbishop of Tuam.

Sympathy

At a meeting of the Tuam District Council held in April 1923 at the Court House, the following resolutions were passed:

No. 1: A vote of sympathy with the relatives of the prisoners recently executed in Tuam.

No. 2: A vote of condolence with their colleague Mr Martin Higgins whose brother was killed in action against the Free State army at Headford.

Mr T. Costello, DC, referring to the Tuam executions, said that was the first time since the days of Cromwell that executions were carried out in Tuam. He did not know why the men were taken to Tuam for execution except it was to make the volleys ring in the ears of the Archbishop of Tuam or perhaps the Free State meeting held a few days ago was such a failure that it became necessary to bring something into the town to strike terror into the people. The sword would never succeed in this country. It had been tried by England for 800 years; she had also tried the gibbet, the jack and the rack and all and each failed, and today she was like Pontius Pilate, she had washed her hands out of the Irish trouble. Ireland could not afford to lose the men who had been sacrificed on both sides and he thought it was their duty to call on their representatives to resign, as they had not the consent of the people to carry out executions.

THE SIX EXECUTIONS IN TUAM were the largest number of IRA prisoners to be put to death in one centre since seven (Stephen White, Joseph Johnston, Patrick Mangan, Patrick Nolan, Brian Moore, James O'Connor and Patrick Bagnel) had been shot in Dublin, just before Christmas on 19 December 1922. They also brought the total placed before firing squads by the Free State authorities to 71. Given that they were all locals and that they were shot, rather unexpectedly, in the smallish town of Tuam in the heart of rural Connacht, the impact was enormous. Frequently, there have been suggestions that the executions were arranged for the Tuam workhouse rather than Renmore barracks in Galway because the Catholic bishop of Galway had just died, about that time and General Mulcahy in particular, a practising Catholic all his life, could not tolerate the idea of blood-letting in the city while the bishop was being mourned.

The attack on Headford, two days previously, sealed the fate of the six men who had been in custody for almost two months, and had been sentenced to death 'on hold' like many others at the time. Free State apologists will claim that the decision to execute 'was the fault' of those who remained active outside the prisons. Republican apologists suspect that certain members of the Free State command in the west had also to be forced to taste execution blood and half a dozen executions in an area like Tuam would frighten all but convinced Republicans that the cause was not worth the risk. Some Republicans even go so far as to suggest that the line-up in the Free State firing squad in Tuam was interesting, that some people were brought in from Mayo – to spread the fear and the involvement of all – including some officers of northern origins. Be that as it may, the reality was that by mid-April 1923 the Civil War was almost over and the ceasefire announcement came into force on 30 April 1923.

I am always amused when I hear people suggesting they do not really understand the relationship between Sinn Féin and the IRA in Irish political history. Republican veterans, De Valera and Aiken, invented the arrangement in those difficult times. For while it was Éamon De Valera, as President of Sinn Féin and the *de jure* Republic which had only been disestablished by force of arms, who announced the cessation of hostilities, it was Frank Aiken and the IRA Council which took the decision separately, and then informed Dev, who was not on the Army Council, of the decision. This was a cessation of hostilities, not a surrender of the Republican position, much less a hand-over of arms or even a 'decommissioning'. Dev told his followers, as did Aiken, to 'dump arms', to keep them in a safe place, because they might be needed again at a later date.

PERHAPS THE BEST FORM OF 'decommissioning' was, and is, rust. Certainly, the Republican leadership of 1923 who defected to the new Fianna Fáil by 1926, never asked the IRA rank and file, who had sacrificed so much in the Civil War, to go back to their dumped arms again. In fact, even though the IRA played a significant part in helping Fianna Fáil to win power in the 1932 general election, within another decade the De Valera government was accused of shooting, hanging and interning former Republican comrades who did not join them in 1926. These were the Republicans who regarded Dev's 1937 Constitution solution as another 'Stepping Stone' that would not work either, because it was based on faulty foundations. It may be worth adding here that it was not the oath, as such, that caused the main problem for Republicans in the 1920s, but what it stood for – British sovereignty over Ireland and the right to rule in any part of Ireland.

EXECUTIONS AFTER CEASEFIRE

WHILE THE SIX EXECUTIONS IN Tuam on 11 April 1923 brought the total of the Civil War to 71, six more were to be added to the infamous total of '77' before it was all over.

On 25 April 1923 three men – Edward Greaney, James McInerney and Reginald Hathaway – were shot in Tralee. Hathaway was a former British soldier who deserted to the Irish Republican cause because he was convinced of its righteousness. When the split came, he took the anti-Treaty IRA side and fought with courage in West Cork and South Kerry. It was unfortunate that he was executed the day before Frank Aiken announced the cessation of hostilities that came into effect on 30 April 1923. The same could be said for Patrick Mahoney who was shot in Ennis the following morning, 26 April 1923.

But even the end of the fighting did not persuade the Free State authorities to desist from further 'official executions'. Chris Quinn and William Shaughnessy went before yet another firing squad on 2 May 1923, thus pushing the grand total from 75 to 77 in a manner that seems to suggest, once again, that those at the top of the Army Council of the new state wanted to involve as many Free State army commands as possible in the blood-letting. Nor did it end there. Further 'unofficial executions' followed, the most famous one being that of Captain Noel Lemass who was seized by government forces in Dublin on 3 July 1923. It was understood that he had been snatched by the new Special Branch interrogators based in Oriel House, but nothing further was heard about him until his mutilated body was found in the Dublin Mountains on 12 October 1923.

The capture and, it was accepted, the torture of Noel Lemass remains a cause of rumour and speculation to this very day. He is remembered by a later generation for the fact that his younger brother, Seán Lemass, who was also out in 1916, like W. T. Cosgrave, never mentioned the matter in public or sought to make political capital out of it as he made his way up the Fianna Fáil ladder to become Taoiseach. But there are rumours that 'Lemass was one of those who knew too much'. In other words, some Free State opponents in the Civil War intended to silence him, even if there was a ceasefire, and the war was over. It has also been suggested by some sources that Lemass may have been involved in the unofficial attack on Seán Hales and Pádraic Ó Máille on 7 December 1922 which was used by the Cosgrave government as an excuse for the shooting without trial of Rory, Liam, Dick and Joe the following morning. Or at least that he knew too much about who was really involved in an incident which the IRA never claimed and never sanctioned.

Whatever about all this, the point needs to be made clearly that Liam Lynch never suggested that all elected TDs be attacked or shot. Hales and Ó Máille were on the IRA 'hit list' at the time because they voted for the Emergency Powers provisions of the Provisional Parliament which removed the power to inflict death from the courts and indeed from the government and handed it over to a three-man military council (where Defence Minister Mulcahy doubled as Commander-in-Chief) which could order an execution without appeal or sanction. It may be difficult for some of us to comprehend today how it was possible to arrive at such manifestly unjust ways of doing things in the new Irish Free State whose supporters said they were fighting for democracy. The reality is that it is weak uncertain governments, not strong ones, that behave like this. For those who ask why no legal redress was taken for all the official misdeeds, including 'official executions' of the Civil War, an Indemnity Bill was passed on 3 August 1923 to protect the forces of the Free State government from the consequences of actions taken by them against Republicans.

LET US AGAIN RETURN TO the last of the notes compiled by J. J. Waldron about the aftermath of the Tuam executions and indeed the entire sad saga of Civil War in the Galway area.

Under the heading *The Aftermath,* he writes: The day came when the military vacated the Tuam workhouse and returned to their headquarters, Athlone, taking with them the exhumed bodies of the executed men and later re-interring them in Athlone.

In the meantime, the policy of the then government was to abolish the task of the workhouses, which included the one in Glenamaddy which catered for the children.

These latter were eventually transferred to Tuam. They were under the care of the Bon Secours sisters and the sister in charge was one of the finest nuns I have ever met, named Mother Hortens. She did a marvellous job in renovating the Tuam workhouse and in 12 months the children had a home from home. She did a very charitable act too in marking the site where the Republican boys were executed in 1923 and later had a glass protection erected around it, and a beautiful old Crucifix placed on the wall. She was also responsible for the founding of the present fine hospital in Vicar Street, which, down the years, has expanded beyond all expectations.

In the meantime, as the days passed, the relatives of the executed men were demanding the return of the bodies of the young men to be buried in their parish. They eventually succeeded in their demand, and one day, the relatives and friends had the satisfaction of bringing them back and having them interred in Downapatrick Graveyard in a communal grave. Today if you visit there you can't help noticing a tall granite pillar with a cross over their grave and their names inscribed on a plaque underneath. This was placed there by their comrades and friends to show to the world that they fought, they have departed to a better world and they will never be forgotten. The design of the monument was suggested by their Republican comrades, first by Mr John Heneghan of Athenry Road,

Tuam and later carried out by Mr Mick Martin, BE, Taylor's Hill, Galway.

Since these events previously narrated took place, it's 50 years ago. Unbelievable changes have taken place in the country, its face has been lifted, as it were, and signs of prosperity appear all around us The old workhouse is gone with its jail-like surrounding walls. And in its place houses are appearing where people will dwell, and the happy cries of children will be heard in play, and so life carries on. At the request of the special organising committee, the County Council has assented to leave the oratory standing to be turned into a community centre, and will carry out some necessary repairs on it.

Another item is, also, that the Archbishop of Tuam has given permission for an annual Mass to be said for the souls of the executed men and those that died there during the Famine.

Go ndéana Dia trócaire ar a n-anamacha.

There are a few other outstanding notes:

Week of May 10th, 1923
Troops searching the Headford district captured a well-known Republican Mr Martin Kyne of Caherlistrane. In his house they discovered dispatches, field-glasses, trench coats and many other articles of use to the Republican forces.

In the home of another Republican Martin Rooney they collected a shot gun, cartridges, together with a quantity of cigarettes and tobacco and he was arrested also.

In the same district, three other Republicans from Barrack Street, Tuam were arrested, namely Edward Hayes, John Conry and Luke Reilly.

June 11th, 1923
It is rumoured that Mr Tom Maguire, TD, the leader of the Republicans has escaped from Athlone prison, plus an O'Grady and a

Before the great divide – photograph taken in the first weeks of 1922, when three from both sides came together to try to prevent a civil war. [L to r] Seán Mac Eoin, Seán Moylan, Eoin O'Duffy, Liam Lynch, Gearóid O'Sullivan and Liam Mellows. Mac Eoin, O'Duffy and O'Sullivan were pro-Treaty, while Moylan, Lynch and Mellows stood by the Republic. Lynch, who became chief-of-staff of the IRA, was killed in action in April 1923. Mellows was one of the four executed by order of the Free State government, while a prisoner in Mountjoy, on 8 December 1922. Moylan served as a TD for North Cork and as Minister for Lands, Education and Agriculture in De Valera governments in the 1940s and 1950s. He died in November 1957.

Pictured at the historic take-over of Renmore Military Barracks on 7 February 1922. The pencilled caption in Irish on the back of the photograph reads as follows: 'Tógaint seilbhe ar Dhún na Rinne Móire ag Arm Phoblacht na hÉireann ó fhórsaí Shasana 7 Feabhra 1922. Garda den 4ú Cath, 2ú Briogáid, 1ú Roinn an iarthair. An chéad Garda sa Dún [ag féachaint orthu ó clé go deas]: Annraí Ó Loingsigh, Seán Ó Brannagáin, Seán Ó Ceannabháin, Pádraig de Faoite, Micheál Mac Proinnsias, Seosamh Ó Ceallaigh, Pádraig Ó Feinndhe. An Sairgint Tomás Ó Ceallaigh i gceannas an Garda'. It is signed by T. Mac Cormaic. No other details are given. (Le caoinchead B. Mhic Ghabhainn)

An IRA firing party rendering honours at the grave of Louis Darcy in Clydiagh Cemetery, Co. Galway, during the Truce on 1921.

Comdt Louis Darcy, OC Headford Battalion IRA, killed by British forces at Merlin, Co. Galway on 24 March 1921.

Volunteer Dan McCormack, Milltown, Co Galway died on 15 August 1929 from wounds received on the attack on Headford Barracks on 9 April 1923. He lost his left arm above the elbow and his right leg below the knee. The mark on his chin was from the exit wound.

North Galway Brigade I.R.A.

**CAPT.
MICHAEL WALSH**

**Derrymore,
Caherlistrane.**

Executed at Athlone
on January 20th, 1923

Comdt. P. Cunnane O.C.

They gave
their Lives
for the
Republic.

Lt. Sean Maguire.

Comdt. Martin Burke.

Lt. & Q.M. Stephen Joyce.

Vol. Seamus O' Maille.

Lt.- Comdt. Thomas Hughes.

Lt. & Q.M. Sean Newell.

Vol. Hubert Collins.

Vol. Martin Moylan.

Vol. Michael Monaghan

Remains of the executed Volunteers, lying overnight in St Mary's church, Headford, Co. Galway, 28–29 October 1924. (Photo: Frank Glynn, Milltown, Co. Galway)

From memorial card of Reginald Dunne and Joseph O'Sullivan. They were arrested for the assassination of Sir Henry Wilson, sentenced to death and hanged in Wandsworth Gaol on 10 August 1922. The following appeared on the back of the memorial card: 'All members of the IRA operating in Britain belonged to the Army of the Republic and received their orders from GHQ, Dublin. When the order for the execution of an enemy of Ireland arrived both of these brave men volunteered to carry it out. This they did most successfully at very short notice ...'

The Men of the West: Michael Kilroy's IRA Column [Fourth Western], taken on the southern slopes of Mount Nephin, Co. Mayo at 11.15 p.m. on 21 June 1921: Back row [l to r]: M. Kilroy, T. Ketterick, E. Moane, J. Gibbons, J. Walsh, P. J. Cannon, P. Lambert, J. Kelly, J. Doherty, B. Malone, J. Rush, J. Ring. Middle row: M. Naughton, J. Hogan, J. Hearney, D. Simmon, J. Keane, J. Connolly, R. Joyce, P. McNamara, W. Malone. Front row: G. Gavin, T. Heavey, J. Duffy, J. McDonagh, P. Kelly, J. Moran, J. Flaherty, B. Cryan, M. Staunton. In front: *Dr. J. A. Madden.* (Photo: J. J. Leonard and Son, Bofeenaun, Ballina, Co. Mayo)

The last appearance of Liam Mellows – giving the oration at the annual Republican commemoration at the grave of Wolfe Tone, Bodenstown, Co. Kildare in June 1922.

West Connemara Brigade, IRA Flying Column 1921 [First Battalion Leenane, Second Battalion Ros Muc, Third Battalion Roundstone, Fourth Battalion Clifden]. **Front row [l to r]:** *P. J. McDonnell, Brigade OC, Staff Capt. C. Breen, Staff Capt. R. Joyce, G. Staunton, Vice Comdt. Second Battalion, G. Bartley, OC Fourth Battalion, J. King, OC Third Battalion, M. Conneely, Brigade Adj., M. Conroy, Quartermaster Third Battalion, J. Feehan, Brigade Quartermaster.* **Back Row:** *Vol. J. Mannion, Lt J. Conneely, Vol. J. King, Third Battalion, Staff Capt. P. Bartley, Fourth Battalion, J. Dundass, Adj., Third Battalion, Patrick Wallace, Quartermaster, First Battalion, Vol. W. King, First Battalion, Vol. P. Wallace, First Battalion, Vol. T. Madden, Fourth Battalion, J. C. King Adj. First Battalion, Capt. D. Keane, Third Battalion, Lt T. Coyne, First Battalion.* (Photo: J. J. Leonard and Son, Bofeenaun, Ballina, Co. Mayo)

Comdt General Tom Maguire [1921], TDÉ and GOC Second Western Division IRA. His brother Seán [17] was one of the six Volunteers executed in Tuam on 11 April 1923.

Why reckon the pangs that
have sufficed,
*Star of the Morning, Mary,
come,*
To bring free souls to their
Captain, Christ?
*Mary Immaculate, guide them
home.*

Rory and Liam are dead and
gone,
*Star of the Morning, Mary,
come,*
They have found the lights
that go out at dawn,
*Mary Immaculate, guide them
home.*

Rory and Liam and Dick and
Joe,
*Star of the Morning, Mary,
come,*
Our starlight fades, but the
road they know,
*Mary Immaculate, guide them
home.*

Pádraig de Brún.

In Memoriam
**Rory O'Connor,
Liam Mellowes,
Richard Barrett,
Joseph McKelvey,**
Pro Patria Mortuorum in Carcere
Mountjoy
In Festo Immaculatae Conceptionis
B. V. M.
Die 8° Decembris, 1922
Requiescant in Pace.

Rory and Liam are dead and
gone,
*Star of the Morning, Mary,
come,*
Slain at the Eighth of December's dawn,
*Mary Immaculate, guide them
home.*

Rory and Liam and Dick and
Joe,
*Star of the Morning, Mary,
come,*
Red is their hearts' blood, their
souls like snow,
*Mary Immaculate, guide them
home.*

Their slayers have rung no
passing bell,
*Star of the Morning, Mary,
come,*
But the rifles' crack is their
funeral knell,
*Mary Immaculate, guide them
home.*

Their eyes are steady in face
of Death,
*Star of the Morning, Mary,
come,*
For their minds are rapt by
the vision of faith,
*Mary Immaculate, guide them
home.*

For Winter will pass and
Spring be born,
*Star of the Morning, Mary,
come,*
And Freedom will waken the
land at morn,
*Mary Immaculate, guide them
home.*

And what is Death but an
envoy sped,
*Star of the Morning, Mary,
come,*
With a call from the Heaven
of Ireland's dead?
*Mary Immaculate, guide them
home.*

*Memorial card for Rory O'Connor, Liam Mellows, Richard Barrett and Joseph McKelvey – executed on
8 December 1922. Verse on mortuary card written by Mon. Pádraig de Brún.*

Photograph taken at Easter 1928 following a meeting of the Second [All-Ireland] Dáil Éireann elected in 1921 and never dissolved. Even after the defection of Fianna Fáil the previous year there was still a quorum present to conduct business.

Front row: *Phil Shanahan [Dublin Mid], Prof. W. F. P. Stockley [NUI], Kate O'Callaghan [Limerick City and Limerick East], Art O'Connor [Kildare and Wicklow], J. J. O'Kelly [Louth and Meath], Mary MacSwiney [Cork City], Dáithí Ceannt [Cork North-East and East], George Count Plunkett [Leitrim and Roscommon], Brian O'Higgins [Clare].*
Second row: *Count O'Byrne [Tipperary South, North and Mid], Éamonn Dee [Waterford], Séamus Lennon [Carlow and Kilkenny], M. P. Colivet [Limerick City and Limerick East], Austin Stack {Kerry and West Limerick], Charles Murphy [Dublin South], Seán O'Mahony [Fermanagh and Tyrone], Ada English [NUI], Thomas O'Donoghue [Kerry and West Limerick], J. Crowley [Mayo North and West].*
Back row: *Thomas Maguire [Mayo South and Roscommon South], Seán MacSwiney [Co. Cork West, South and Mid], Seán O'Farrell [Sligo and Leitrim], Brian Mellows [Galway], Caitlín Brugha [Waterford], Eileen Tubbard, stenographer and Dublin City Councillor Joe Clarke, courier. Seán O'Farrell, Brian Mellows and Caitlín Brugha, having been elected in 1923, were not members of the Second Dáil Éireann.* (Photo: Seán Maguire)

man named Pender, an active Republican, from Ballinasloe with 12 or 14 others.

The course adopted to effect their liberty was by getting possession of army uniforms.

Maguire was arrested in Headford about six months ago.

June 25th, 1923

It is stated that things are coming back to normal in the area of Headford and its surroundings after the disturbances from some time past. Business is rapidly improving in the town.

The traders suffered severely with the shootings and riots. The only bank in town, the National, had to close down when its premises was destroyed, but now they are carrying on from a temporary site.

It is of historic interest to look back and read the list of claims made by the landlords of the period for the burning of their mansions, etc., during the Civil War. It gives one some idea of the size of their property and the value they held 50 years ago. Most of it now is divided up amongst the tenants.

These were the claim amounts at the Quarter Sessions in September, 1923. The value today (1972) would probably be three times the claim. The combined total amounts to £153,779-14-4:

Col Lewen, Castlegrove House and Lodge, £65,839; Col Bernard, Castlehacket, House and Lodge, £56,358; James Greated, Lydican Castle, Claregalway, £8,192; Bodkin & Hoade, Annagh House, Ballyglunin, £3,790; Weldon, Coolarne, Athenry, £1,647; Concannon & St George, Tyrone House, £4,000; McDonnell, Ballykeeran Lodge, Glasson, £1,660; Gleeson, Dunmore, damage to Courthouse, £590; Gilmore, Glenamaddy, Sawmill at Patch, £1,400; O'Malley, Dunmore, car, petrol, etc., £540; Kirwan, Dalgin, Motor Car, £300; O'Driscoll, Tuam, damage to RIC barracks, Mountbellew, £2,000; Rooney, Tuam, damage to cars and bicycles, £723 and O'Rorke, Clonberne, motor car, £400.

CLEARLY, WITH THE CONDUCT OF Quarter Sessions and the filing of claims, the mood of the country was settling down to one of resignation to the new order – 'the Greengrocers' Republic' as Frank O'Connor, himself an IRA activist during the Civil War in Cork, called it.

Others said it was a withdrawal from 'anarchy' – the type of revolutionary 'anarchy' they had all participated in during the Black and Tan era from 1919 to 1921. Some, like Pádraic Ó Máille, quickly came to realise that it was not the 'Stepping Stone' Collins had said it was, when he used his position as head of the secret IRB, to push through the Treaty vote on the basis that 'what is good enough for Mick Collins, is good enough for us'. Ó Máille had the courage to resign from Cumann na nGaedheal, with nine others, and paid a price for doing so.

On the other hand, when De Valera, humiliated and defeated, picked himself up and changed his political tack with the new Fianna Fáil party (which owed most of the organisation work to Seán Lemass and Gerry Boland) he admitted, in later life, that he had greater freedom under the Treaty than he anticipated, and that much of this was due to the way the first Free State government under W. T. Cosgrave and Kevin O'Higgins had laboured in the most appallingly difficult circumstances. Others, of course, like Tom Maguire never deviated. Dev, after he failed to get his way in Sinn Féin in 1925, stated on the record of the Dáil that 'there are those outside this house who can claim the same continuity and commitment to the Republican idea that we did up to 1925'.

The rights and wrongs of this terrible period in our history are of concern because, as is clear each passing day, we have failed to resolve not only the problem that caused it, but indeed the problems arising from its legacy. Those who claim that 'the politics of the Civil War are gone' have not only pulled down the blinkers on the agony that continues north of the border, they ignore the stark reality of the extent to which that same 'Northern' or 'National' or

'British' problem damages all other activities in this country/island/state. They also ignore the enormous cost and misery, never mind loss of lives, that it imposes even on those of us here in the south who have fairly successfully isolated ourselves from the raw reality.

One point that needs to be made about the Civil War in Galway, or anywhere else, is that we bear its tragedy and its lessons constantly in mind. Such an appalling vista must never be allowed to happen again and the surest way to avoid that danger, and to tackle the contradictions it presents for all sides, is to make sure there is open and honest, fresh and original discussion about it.

RETURN OF BODIES TO RELATIVES
OCTOBER 1924

IT MAY BE OF INTEREST TO note that in the version of the Frank Cunnane letter printed in *Eleven Galway Martyrs* in 1985 the address is given as 'in the Reception Ward, Galway Gaol, 1923' rather than Tuam workhouse. This adds to the significance of the *Connacht Tribune* report of the following Saturday 14 April 1923, quoted in the 1985 account, which also stated: 'On Monday morning (9.4.'23), the Bishop of Galway, Dr O'Dea died and so followed a period of mourning which lasted until his funeral on Thursday, April 12th. On Tuesday, John Higgins was buried in Kilbannon Cemetery after Mass in Tuam. The same day, six men were taken aside in Galway Jail and told they would be executed at 8.00 a.m. the next day, not in Galway, but in Tuam workhouse'. It then lists the six volunteers and continues 'They were brought from Galway to Tuam workhouse that evening. They wrote their final letters, got Mass and in two groups of three, lined up by the Oratory Wall and were executed early on April 11th, 1923.' The *Connacht Tribune* of the following Saturday, 14 April, along with details of the bishop's funeral, in Galway, describes the events in Tuam as follows: 'The condemned men, it is stated, went to their doom firmly and with brave hearts. They had been attended during the night by two of the town priests and in the morning heard Mass, at which two of them served. The priests were with them to the last.

'The news of the executions cast a gloom over the people who could hardly realise what awful happening had taken place in their midst that morning. About 8.00 a.m. two volleys were fired and it is stated that the condemned men were taken out in parties of three each, and blindfolded and their hands joined as in prayer. They had prayed fervently during the night before and in the morning and were fully consoled, prepared to meet their Creator. The six bodies, enclosed in six coffins were interred in the ground within the barracks and it is stated that the ground was consecrated. No official information of the executions would be issued to the press.'

When the Free State Army vacated the Tuam workhouse towards the end of 1923, they exhumed the bodies of the six and brought them to Athlone, headquarters of the Western Command of the new triumphant Free State 'National Army'. This was greatly resented, but all requests to return the bodies to the relatives were ignored by the Cosgrave government until the autumn of 1924 when, faced with a number of by-elections, throughout the state, it was decided to hand back the remains of all 77 who had been shot on the orders of the Free State Army Council, independent of all judicial or even political control, during the Civil War. Those who seek to vilify Liam Lynch and other IRA leaders and who suggest that shooting on sight was the only answer to those who engaged in such highly irregular conduct, even by the normal rules of warfare, should recall that those 'democrats' who handed over the powers to the army at that time – and before the Irish Free State was even founded – were effectively washing their hands of the responsibility they themselves said they had as a Provisional Government and parliament, and handing it over to a three-man junta. Any two members of the Army Council could sanction the execution of anybody they did not like. Erskine Childers is the saddest example of this, not only because of the shameful way he was put to death before his appeal to the high court was even considered, but also because the propaganda against the 'damned Englishman' who had converted to the Republican cause, was so blind and prejudiced as to give us an insight into the real outlook of the pro-Free State mind at the time.

We get another insight into that mind when the return of the bodies was finally brought to the attention of the Cosgrave government in June 1924. On the twenty-seventh of that month, in a confidential letter to the Free State President, the Commander of the Free

State Army, General Eoin O'Duffy wrote:

> The re-interment of an executed irregular would, almost to a certainty, be made the occasion for a demonstration for the purposes of attracting the sympathies of the general public towards the bereavement of the relatives, at a time when the necessity *(sic)* for the executions has, to a certain extent, been faded from the minds of the people.

Since many of the posts occupied by the Free State during the Civil War had been abandoned again, General O'Duffy suggested that: 'It is necessary that the remains of executed irregulars interred therein, should be exhumed and re-interred at the nearest permanent post.' He added 'With reference to the two bodies interred in Waterford Prison, and the one in Cork Prison, it is necessary that these should be raised and coffined.' O'Duffy's suggestions were accepted by the Free State cabinet, but the prospect of defeat in by-elections later on that year prompted the secretary of Cumann na nGaedheal to write to Cosgrave on 16 September 1924, not only about economic and administrative factors, but also about the Civil War legacy. He wrote: 'In these circumstances the Coiste Gnótha believed that the Ministry of Defence must surely have had good and sufficient reasons for their action in digging up the remains of recently executed men at Tuam and elsewhere and unceremoniously disposing of them in some fashion which can only have been unsatisfactory to the official who gave the order, but which has certainly produced violent indignation amongst even our own members and is regarded throughout the country, as nothing short of an atrocity.

'The Coiste Gnótha feel the political effect of this measure all the more keenly ... when the same department disinterred the bodies of certain British soldiers in Cork, about the same time, the public, on whom we and the government depend, were able to read in the papers a full account of the very proper treatment meted out to the remains on this occasion. The contrast has been bitterly commented on throughout the country, but nowhere more than in Cork, where we are saddled with the task of winning two important by-elections.' Clearly, the significance of by-elections as a pressure-point on government was already becoming clear in the Irish Free State. Under the multi-seat PR system, constituencies do not lose their entire Dáil voice on the death of a TD, and the habit of holding by-elections, as in Britain (because a dead MP means no voice in parliament for a certain constituency), was deemed to be unsuitable mainly because such campaigns in multi-seat areas, only led to distraction for an elected government. In order to counter the damage already done, the Cumann na nGaedheal government finally decided, in October 1924, to release the bodies of the executed Republicans to their families. They took 'special precautions to ensure that arms would not be carried by body-guards at the funerals and no firing parties were to be allowed.'

On 28 October 1924, the Free State released 20 bodies – those executed at Tuam, Athlone, Drumboe, Co. Donegal and Birr – through the back gate of Custume barracks in Athlone at ten minute intervals. Séamus Ó Maille was taken to Uachtar Ard and was buried later in Cill Choimin Cemetery. Thomas Hughes was buried in Cornamagh Cemetery near Athlone. The *Connacht Tribune* (1 November 1924) described the funerals in North Galway as follows: 'it was nearly 12 o'clock (midnight) on Tuesday night when the procession arrived in Tuam. It was the saddest funeral procession ever seen or ever likely to be seen in the country. Over 20 motor cars were in the procession – the first nine containing the remains of the deceased and the relatives followed in cars. The coffins were draped with the Republican Tricolour. There was a shell coffin in each case, covering the coffin in which the remains were placed at the time of the execution.

'In Tuam a large crowd remained on the streets awaiting the arrival of the funeral and though there was a heavy downpour of rain, and the remains did not arrive until 11.30 p.m. the people stood waiting. As the funeral cars drove slowly through the town heads were uncovered and soldiers and civic guards saluted. Spanning some of the principal streets were streamers with mourning crosses in Republican colours.

'There was no delay in Tuam and all the cars proceeded on to Headford where they arrived at 1.30 a.m. On passing Belclare church the bell tolled, thus lending a solemn sadness to the countryside around, at the late hour of night. The remains were left in Headford church where the rosary was recited.

'A North Galway IRA Brigade stood guard throughout the night.' The report states however that 'the remains of John McGuire, brother of T. McGuire, TD, were conveyed to Cross, Cong from where they were taken, after High Mass on Thursday, and interred with the other coffins in the Republican plot at Donoghpatrick Burial Ground. The interment took place after 11.00 a.m. Mass on Thursday, October 30th, 1924. Arrangements were made to hold a general day of mourning in Tuam and surrounding towns by having all business suspended during the day.'

It should be recalled that in the five by-elections then held in November 1924, Cumann na nGaedheal won three, in Donegal, Cork East and Cork Borough. But they lost North Mayo, where Republican John A. Madden defeated Michael Tierney (the Cumann na nGaedheal native of East Galway who later became president of UCD and was married to Eoin MacNeill's daughter) by 14,628 votes to 13,758, while in Dublin South, Seán F. Lemass, 1916 veteran, and brother of the murdered Noel Lemass, took the seat for Sinn Féin with 17,297 votes to 16,340 for Seamus Hughes of Cumann na nGaedheal.

We should also stress that the Cumann na nGaedheal party was in fact founded not before, but at the end of the Civil War. We have shown, I hope, how the Civil War victory was achieved, not by politics, but by the more aggressive Free State army policies, acting without political restrictions. Cumann na nGaedheal, the political party, back to which Fine Gael traces its roots, was not founded until 27 April 1923 – that is the day after General Frank

Aiken, the new Chief-of-Staff of the IRA, issued the ceasefire order which came into effect at midday on 30 April 1923. In spite of the ceasefire, however, the Free State army proceeded with the execution of the final two Republicans of the famous '77', Chris Quinn and William Shaughnessy in Ennis on 2 May 1923. Going ahead with further executions a few days after the conflict had been ended, is only one other reason why Clare has had such a bitter Civil War legacy ever since. It also probably secured Mr De Valera's support in Clare for the rest of his life, and is perhaps part of the reason why his grand-daughter, Síle de Valera, represents Clare.

When Cumann na nGaedheal came together as a party at the end of the Civil War, there was little doubt about who the leader would be. William T. Cosgrave, the modest Dubliner who stood in for both Collins and Griffith, after both died within ten days of each other in August 1922, and forced the Free State through the bloody Civil War months that followed, was the unanimous choice as party leader. But the first President of Cumann na nGaedheal was Eoin MacNeill, of the Glens of Antrim, the man who helped found both Conradh na Gaeilge in 1893, and the Irish Volunteers in 1913, the man who tried to call off the 1916 Rising, who was a TD for Derry city in the first 32 county Dáil, and who shared the Clare multi-seat constituency with De Valera and Brian O'Higgins in the new Free State. MacNeill's son Brian was killed on the Republican side in the Civil War, and Eoin's demise as a politician came about after the failure of the Boundary Commission in 1925. What an amazingly complex life he led!

POLITICAL OPPOSITION TO THE FREE STATE CONTINUES

ONE OF THE MOST IMPRESSIVE things about the Irish Republican struggle from 1916 onwards was the way in which various shades of Irish nationalism, from the IRB to the re-organised Sinn Féin after its 1917 Ardfheis, insisted on both a political and a military movement, separate in organisation and structures, but sharing the same ideals and principles. Hence, the elaborate efforts made to endorse the Republican stand of 1916 through Sinn Féin participation in the December 1918 general election. And the equally clear efforts that were made almost immediately by the victorious Sinn Féin elected members to boycott Westminster and proceed with Arthur Griffith's policy of establishing a parliament for all the Irish people at home – Dáil Éireann, Dáil uile Éireann, to which all shades of Irish political opinion were invited. They sought to make Irish self-government as immediate a reality as the circumstances of the time would permit. One of the first priorities of this new Republican Dáil Éireann was to seek international recognition for Ireland, as an independent sovereign state (whether termed 'Poblacht' or 'Saorstát') particularly by trying to get recognition for Ireland's case at the post-World War Peace Conference at Versailles. The Dáil also sought to show to the world that Ireland's right to nationhood was reflected in a separate language and unique cultural tradition that dated back further than most of those in central and eastern Europe, for example, that were making a claim for nationhood on the same basis at the time. The first meeting of Dáil Éireann did not go through the motions of the *cúpla focal*, but conducted its business before the world in Irish, despite the odds, and despite the reality that centuries of alien government and a West British educational system ('the murder machine' as Pádraig Pearse called it) meant that Irish persons, including those in the professions and in positions of influence, were unable to speak the national language. Since 1893 when it was founded, Conradh na Gaeilge, had advanced the cause of Irish, and enhanced its status in particular in educational circles, and most especially since 1908 when it won the battle to have Irish recognised as an essential subject for those who wished to matriculate in the new National University of Ireland (NUI – Ollscoil na hÉireann). The genuine recognition and support which the First Dáil Éireann gave to the national language was significant. It was also a clear indication of the degree to which Gaelic League thinking, and training provided by Conradh na Gaeilge in its cultural battles, had influenced Ireland's struggle for nationhood in the twentieth century and it also explained why so many of 'those who had been at school to the Gaelic League' (to quote Daniel Corkery at a later stage) played such a prominent part in the establishment and workings of the Dáil – the new revolutionary parliament of the Irish Republic.

This close link between the Gaelic revival and the national liberation movement was one of the few things that survived the tragic Civil War split of 1922. It was spelled out in 1931 by Douglas Hyde, first President of Conradh na Gaeilge, in the Introduction to his book *Mise agus an Connradh*, i.e., after the Free State was firmly established, and a year before the Cumann na nGaedheal Government of W. T. Cosgrave was replaced by De Valera and his Fianna Fáil party. Those who claim that the Gaelic League 'was taken over by extremists' in 1915, when Hyde resigned from the presidency, would do well to read his 1931 remarks. While it is true that Hyde took a backseat after 1915, and pursued a distinguished academic career in UCD, it is also true that he re-emerged into Irish public life in 1938 as first President of Ireland under the 1937 Bunreacht na hÉireann with all-party consent. Nowhere was the almost unanimous agreement on the importance of linguistic and cultural self-reliance in the national movement to be seen as in the way the Irish revival policies survived the 1922 split. In the decade which followed the basic building blocks of saving the language, conserving the Gaeltacht and providing all citizens with a basic knowledge of their linguistic and cultural heritage through the educational system, were laid down by the Free State government and Cumann na nGaedheal ministers like Earnán de Blaghid (Ernest Blythe) a northern Protestant, and Richard Mulcahy, a southern Catholic. Both were admired even by their most bitter Republican critics, because of their work for the language in difficult circumstances, when lack of resources, and indeed lack of education and linguistic revival experiences and research were things that most of the world were still unaware of.

I have outlined [pages 147–148] the story of Irish elections from 1918 to 1923 when, in the wake of the Free State military victory in the field, Cumann na nGaedheal won a fairly easy contest bearing in mind that anything from 10,000 to 15,000 of the most prominent anti-Treaty activists were still in jail. But it was not all good news for the Cumann na nGaedheal government. Anti-Treaty Republicans won 44 seats, up from 36 in the 'Pact' election the previous year, when unfamiliarity with PR meant that only one TD in each constituency was all that those who took the Pact at its word could muster. By August 1923, the lessons of 1922 had been learned by the minority of Republicans still free, and the total of 44 out of the new 26 county Dáil of 153 seats, was impressive against the 63 of the outgoing government, Cumann na nGaedheal. Republicans, even if not in jail, would not attend in Leinster House in any case. The other seats in the first real Free State Dáil (now called the 'Fourth Dáil Éireann' even though it was confined to 26 counties) went to Farmers (15), Labour (14) with 17 Independents.

By the time the next general election was held in the 26 counties, in June 1927, the political scene had changed dramatically. The Boundary Commission had collapsed in November 1925. Dublin negotiated a humiliating 'Final Settlement' of outstanding financial matters arising from the Treaty – but partition remained. This entirely artificial 'National Frontier' was unacceptable, not only because a propaganda exercise was under way to try to get it accepted that 'Ulster' consisted of six of the nine counties of the historic province, but also because everybody realised that in forcing places like Derry city, South Armagh and South Down and the counties of Tyrone and Fermanagh to remain in the UK against their will, the Unionists not only had 'bitten off more than they could chew' but had made it impossible for the local power-base of the Loyalists, from the Orange Order to the B-Specials, in Stormont, to be fair to the Nationalist community. Gerrymander, discrimination, religious intolerance and the suppression of all aspects of Irish identity, even the prohibition of placenames in their proper and correctly spelled Irish forms in areas where this was the will of the local council, were all seen to be necessary if the artificial state whose main outline was drawn on a crude sectarian head-count, was to survive. Even the PR system introduced in 1920 to protect minorities had to go by 1929 – without a whimper or a protest from the new Irish government. Most powermongers in the Free State who had taken the 26 county compromise remained as silent as the British Liberals and Socialists in Westminster, who were, in theory, responsible for 'the good government of Northern Ireland'. They were glad to use the 'internal matter' excuse for fear any wider issues might be raised about the undemocratic nature of partition itself – most importantly, the rigid illiberal voting system which they clung on to in Britain at the time they were prescribing PR for Ireland and other colonies.

Éamon De Valera, having failed to get Sinn Féin to recognise a 26 county Dáil at the end of 1925, emerged as leader of the new Fianna Fáil, Republican Party, which was founded in the La Scala Theatre, Dublin, on 16 May 1926. Described originally by his deputy, Seán Lemass as a 'slightly constitutional party' De Valera was careful to stress on the public record 'that there were those who were with us (Sinn Féin) up to 1925, who can claim the same legitimacy and continuity of political objective'. Fianna Fáil were going to try a new way to achieve the same Republican ideal. The fact that others were on the same road did not mean that Dev would be forced off it. The former Sinn Féin anti-Treaty TDs who followed De Valera in this new departure did not enter Leinster House or take the oath in 1926 though some of them believed all Republican deputies should have gone into the Dáil on a 'once off empty formula' protest at the time of the ratification of the border at the end of 1925, when there was a chance of defeating the Boundary Commission measure and the government, if there was a full house. Others, like Tipperary IRA hero, Dan Breen, decided to enter the Dáil in January 1927 by subscribing to the 'empty formula' – as Dev and his followers would do in August. But Breen was punished by his Fianna Fáil/Republican Party supporters and lost his seat in the June 1927 general election as Fianna Fáil was still an abstentionist party. He returned to Fianna Fáil as a TD in 1932 and served until the 1960s. Other prominent Fianna Fáil ministers, like Seán Moylan (Cork) and Michael Hilliard (Meath), did not enter the 26 county Dáil until De Valera's new government abolished the oath – having come to power via the 'empty formula' route in 1932.

De Valera, who had been in America in the early part of 1927, trying to win support for Fianna Fáil from Irish American leaders and in particular to win some of the Irish-American support funds then being sorted out in court, to help with the cost of setting up a new national daily newspaper, the *Irish Press*, had to rush home in May to take part in the election campaign. Again, the results were encouraging, if somewhat confusing. This is how the 153 seats were shared:

Cumann na nGaedheal	47
Fianna Fáil	44
The Labour Party	22
Independents	14

Farmers	11
National League	8
Sinn Féin	5
Independent Republican Abstentionists	2
Total	153

The choice on offer in larger multi-seat constituencies – anything from 3 to 9 seats per constituency, usually based on a whole county – was being availed of by the electorate and the Dáil now had more deputies belonging to the smaller parties than either of the two main Treaty parties. The Cosgrave government as we have seen (pp. 86–87) abolished the right of constitutional initiative, which De Valera intended to use to force a referendum on the oath, through the collection of signatures of registered voters. Following the assassination of Kevin O'Higgins, Minister for Justice, in July 1927, even more drastic public safety measures were introduced, as well as an Electoral Amendment Bill under which all candidates at parliamentary elections were required, before they could be legally nominated, to swear on affidavit to take the oath of allegiance if elected.

It was in these circumstances that Fianna Fáil deputies, but not the five Sinn Féin TDs, came to 'subscribe' to the oath by signing the book on entry to the Dáil, while at the same time publicly declaring that the entire exercise was merely 'an empty formula', on 12 August 1927. Dev later said that it was the single most difficult decision of his political life and he feared that historians would find it difficult to understand from his point of view. Fianna Fáil's entry into the Free State Dáil changed Irish political history.

The two Independent Republican abstentionist TDs were Daniel Corkery (North Cork) and Arthur Edward Cleary (NUI). The five Sinn Féin TDs, whose opposition to the Free State Dáil was based as much on its origins and failure to provide for north-eastern Ulster representation, as any oath or 'empty formula' were:

Austin Stack, who came second in the seven seat Kerry constituency; John A. Madden, who was elected fourth in the Mayo North four-seater; Caitlín Bhrugha, who came fourth, in her late husband Cathal's Waterford constituency (four-seater), David Rice Kent who came fourth in the five-seat East Cork constituency, and Oscar Traynor who was elected fifth in the Dublin North eight-seater.

This was the last time for three decades that Sinn Féin as a political party contested elections on a nationwide basis. Not only did most Republican activists opt for De Valera's 'new departure' but, it seems, the Fianna Fáil leader had been particularly successful in America in diverting Irish-American financial support towards Fianna Fáil. The entry of Fianna Fáil into the Free State Dáil on 12 August 1927 altered the mathematical balance of a chamber that had been somewhat unreal, in spite of Labour Party efforts to make the Free State parliament work. Within days Labour proposed a vote of no confidence in the government: 'This House is of opinion that the Executive Council has not retained the support of the majority of Dáil Éireann'. Labour were supported by Fianna Fáil and by the National League, a group of mainly former Home Rule supporters, led by Captain Redmond. But one of the League members, Alderman Jinks from Sligo, failed to put in an appearance when the vote was taken and the vote resulted in a tie: 71 for and 71 against. The casting vote of the Ceann Comhairle saved the Cosgrave government. It has been suggested that Fianna Fáil should have supported a minority Labour government, but it would hardly have succeeded. Labour policies were less focused – too radical, yet at the same time too cautious in confronting Britain on issues like the land annuities and because Captain Redmond's group of former Home Rulers, drawn mainly from east-coast farming constituencies, with one or two urban voices, would probably have nothing to do with either party, except to assist in trying to vote Cumann na nGaedheal out of office.

A second general election had to be held in September 1927, when opposition to the Free State was now focused on De Valera's Republican Party. Sinn Féin, exhausted and broken, almost disappeared from the national electoral scene. They continued in local elections but did not make national headlines again for 30 years, when in 1955, they won two of the 12 Westminster seats in the six counties. Two IRA prisoners were returned for Mid-Ulster (Tom Mitchell) and Fermanagh/South Tyrone (Philip Clarke) at the British general election. In 1957, after the IRA border campaign had been under way, Sinn Féin won four seats in the 26 county general election, one in each province. These were John Joe Rice, third out of three in Kerry South, Ruairí Ó Brádaigh third in the Longford-Westmeath five-seater, John Joe McGirl, top of the poll in the Sligo-Leitrim five-seater, and Éineachán Ó hAnnluain, third in the Monaghan three-seater.

Back in 1927 it was clear from the second general election, in September, that the electorate were less than enthused with some of what had transpired after the June poll, and seemed to avoid further PR fragmentation by boosting the two main Treaty parties, once again, as follows:

Cumann na nGaedheal	62
Fianna Fáil	57
Labour	13
Farmers	6
National League	2
Independents	<u>13</u>
Total:	153

For the first time since 1922 all parties were now participating in the 26 county Dáil of Saorstát Éireann, still bound by oath to the British crown and Free State constitution within the parameters of the 1921 Treaty. But things were far from settled, not only because of Dev's new strategy, but also because the Cumann na nGaedheal ministers who still regarded the Treaty as a 'Stepping Stone' were mobilising support within the British empire, that culminated with the Statutes of Westminster in 1931, and the evolution from empire to Commonwealth of Nations.

Cumann na nGaedheal were returned to office in September, 1927, with the support of Farmers and Independents. While their defeat in the 1932 general election reflected their unpopularity for various reasons, during those years, one should not ignore the real constitutional progress made by that 1927–32 government where the final demise of the British empire was concerned.

In January 1932 the general election results were as follows:

Fianna Fáil	72
Cumann na nGaedheal	57
Labour	7
Farmers	5
Independents	<u>12</u>
Total:	153

Within a decade of the defeat and humiliation of the Civil War split, Éamon de Valera, and his closest aides, Seán Lemass, Seán T. Ó Ceallaigh, Seán McEntee, Gerry Boland, Jim Ryan, P. J. Ruttledge, Tomás Ó Deirg and Frank Aiken were now back in government, but in the 26 counties only, and dependent on the Labour Party. Lots of things were expected to change, and many did. Social and economic policies changed, quickly and radically in some cases, but the constitutional priority that Dev gave to issues like the abolition of the oath gave rise to tense politics. De Valera was elected President of the Executive Council of the Free State in March 1932. Within a month he introduced a bill for the removal of the oath of allegiance to the British monarch and though he was opposed by Cumann na nGaedheal, Independent and Farmer deputies, it eventually passed the Dáil by 77 to 69 votes. De Valera was also engaging in an economic war with Britain who closed her ports to Irish exports as soon as the new government, as promised, refused to pay over the land annuities. Because he felt that there should be no ambiguity about the new policy departures, and because he realised further radical constitutional changes would have to be made, in order to dismantle, as far as possible, the 1921 Treaty settlement, Dev called a snap general election at the beginning of 1933, which produced the following result:

Fianna Fáil	77
Cumann na nGaedheal	48
Centre Party	11
Labour	8
Independents	9
Total	153

This was the last time that the original Free State constituencies with a total of 153 seats would be used, and Fianna Fáil with a symbolic 77 seats won a clear majority – the first party to do so since the overwhelming Sinn Féin victories of the early 1920s. Dáil membership was reduced to 138 seats, in the constituency revision of 1935, which produced the following result the first time this model was used in 1937:

Fianna Fáil	69
Fine Gael	48
Labour	13
Independents	8
Total	138

Fianna Fáil retained its majority in the new situation, though not as clearly as is sometimes suggested, following the party's triumph over Blueshirt threats to refuse to pay rates in the 1934 local government elections, and the evolution of Cumann na nGaedheal, the Centre Party and the Blueshirts into the new Fine Gael-United Ireland party. Constitutional change was in the air, with the passing of Bunreacht na hÉireann, in 1937, and De Valera's ongoing political skills and popularity are reflected in the second general election, held before the Second World War, under the 138 seat (26 county) model in July 1938:

The results were as follows:

Fianna Fáil	77
Fine Gael	45
Labour	9
Independents	7
Total	138

By 1938 it was clear that a rising generation of better informed and organised Irish voters, where each man and woman had the vote at the same age, had solidly rejected the 1921 Treaty settlement. It would appear from the declining fortunes of Fine Gael in the following years that even many of those who had backed the 'Stepping Stone' option originally were having second thoughts. They certainly did not show any electoral generosity to W. T. Cosgrave, General Richard Mulcahy, Ernest Blythe, Desmond Fitzgerald and the other former Sinn Féin people who fought so bravely in defence of the Republic from 1919 to 1922. De Valera was leading the people of the 26 counties, but not the six counties, on the high road to the Republic.

But at a time when Sinn Féin is back in the political limelight once again, those who claim that Gerry Adams and Martin McGuinness have sidetracked the 'abstentionism' bug, that first caused De Valera to compromise in 1925, should recall that one of the single most enduring characteristics of Sinn Féin in its various political adventures was the concentration on Dáil and Westminster elections, the 'national parliament' while ignoring any six county gerrymander arrangements or anything to do with the Stormont regime which Gerry Adams and Martin McGuinness helped to undermine in 1972.

It should also be pointed out that Fianna Fáil never really organised itself or contested elections north of the border though individual governments and ministers helped out occasional 'Republican' individuals in the six counties. Pressure to extend Fianna Fáil into the north-east grew at the time of the Civil Rights campaign in the late 1960s. Donegal Minister Neil T. Blaney, a close friend of Nationalist leader Eddie McAteer, was enthusiastic about the idea 'as soon as the people in the north got themselves organised first'. But Mr Blaney parted with official Fianna Fáil after the Arms Crisis of 1970, and apart from some of the H-block election campaigns later on, the idea of a 32 county Independent Fianna Fáil party never got off the ground. It may be worth recalling that Éamon de Valera was an abstentionist Sinn Féin member for the Stormont Parliament back, after partition, in the 1920s. He represented Co. Down in the Second Dáil Éireann, just as Michael Collins was the Sinn Féin candidate for Co. Armagh. Dev was re-elected to Stormont for South Down in 1933, after he had become Head of the Free State Government in Dublin. But the then leader of Fianna Fáil never attended Stormont nor did he seek to enter by taking an oath or 'empty formula', from then until 1938, when he did not seek re-election.

It only remains now to spell out in some detail, as I did in *The Tuam Herald* series, the way in which the people's rejection of the Treaty settlement was reflected, through the Fianna Fáil party, in Co. Galway from 1927 to 1937.

Galway (City and County)   9 *seats*

Electorate 101,256. Quota 5,715. (Numbers on the left indicate final order of election and figures on the right give first preference votes.)

First Preference

1.	Patrick J. Hogan, Cumann na nGaedheal	5,564
2.	Mark Killilea, Fianna Fáil	4,349
7.	Seán Tubridy, Fianna Fáil	4,287
4.	Seán Broderick, Cumann na nGaedheal	3,906
	Joseph William Mongan, Cumann na nGaedheal	3,245
5.	Martin McDonogh, Cumann na nGaedheal	3,244
3.	Frank Fahy, Fianna Fáil	3,150
8.	Thomas P. Powell, Fianna Fáil	3,136
9.	Gilbert Lynch, Labour Party	2,654
	Herbert Charles Mellows, Sinn Féin	2,548
	James J. Nestor, Cumann na nGaedheal	2,433
	Stephen Jordan, Fianna Fáil	2,241
	Bryan Cusack, Fianna Fáil	2,212
	Patrick Lambert, Farmers	2,031
6.	William John Duffy, National League	2,003
	John Cosgrave, National League	1,991
	John McKeague, Cumann na nGaedheal	1,832
	Pádraic Ó Máille, Clann Éireann	1,809
	James McDonnell, National League	1,795
	John W. Ronaldson, Farmers	1,637
	Seamus O'Mulloy, Independent	1,216
	James Reddington, National League	464

Result: Fianna Fáil 4 (Killilea, Fahy, Tubridy and Powell)
Cumann na nGaedheal 3 (Hogan, Broderick, McDonogh)
Labour Party 1 (Lynch)
National League 1 (William J. Duffy)

Galway (City and County)   *9 seats*
Electorate 101,256. Quota 5,966.

1.	Patrick Hogan, Cumann na nGaedheal	6,069
2.	Seán Broderick, Cumann na nGaedheal	5,236
7.	Seán Tubridy, Fianna Fáil	5,126
3.	Martin McDonogh Cumann na nGaedheal	5,007
4.	Frank Fahy, Fianna Fáil	4,780
5.	Mark Killilea, Fianna Fáil	4,675
6.	Thomas P. Powell, Fianna Fáil	4,551
8.	Joseph William Mongan, Cumann na nGaedheal	4,208
	James J. Nestor, Cumann na nGaedheal	3,944
9.	Stephen Jordan, Fianna Fáil	3,448
	Gilbert Lynch, Labour Party	2,912
	Séamus P. Keely, Fianna Fáil	2,898
	Andrew Staunton, Cumann na nGaedheal	2,680
	James Cosgrave, Independent	2,399
	Pádraic Ó Máille, Independent	1,732

Result: Fianna Fáil 5 (Fahy, Killilea, Powell, Tubridy and Jordan). Cumann na nGaedheal 4 (Hogan, Broderick, McDonogh and Mongan).

IN THIS RESULT THE CLEAR anti-Treaty viewpoint in Galway is reflected in the clear-cut 5/4 result between the two parties. Labour and the National League lost seats, and the two new TDs elected were Stephen Jordan, Fianna Fáil and Joseph Mongan, Cumann na nGaedheal. This reflects the overall national trend away from smaller parties, the concentration on a clear Cumann na nGaedheal *v* Fianna Fáil divide, reflecting a return to the key 'constitutional' issues arising from the origins of the two Civil War factions. This was the last time Galway had a Labour TD until Michael D. Higgins finally made it in the new five-seat West Galway constituency in 1981. Pádraic Ó Máille ran as an Independent in the second (September 1927) general election but with even less success than he had in June. This controversial TD for Connemara in the First Dáil Éireann, whose near-assassination on 7 December 1922 was given as one of the excuses for cabinet reprisal executions against Republicans the following morning, joined Fianna Fáil in the early 1930s, but was never elected to the Dáil again.

THE HISTORIC GENERAL ELECTION OF February 1932 saw the triumph of Fianna Fáil and Dev's Republican Party strategy, ten years after the Civil War. It also marked the transfer of power within the Free State system, from the victors to the vanquished in the Civil War conflict. Cumann na nGaedheal never again gained office. They were merged with the Blueshirts and the Centre Party in the mid-1930s – after a rather confused flirtation with admirers of Continental Fascism – as Fine Gael–United Ireland Party but did not get into office until 1948. Fine Gael with 31 seats was the largest grouping in the first inter-party government that also included Labour, National Labour, Clann na Poblachta, Clann na Talmhan and some Farmers and Independents represented in the new cabinet by James Dillon. Dillon had been expelled from Fine Gael in 1940 by Richard Mulcahy because he sought to compromise Irish neutrality during the Second World War. Fine Gael rallied because of its government experience from 1948 to 1951 and James Dillon, who had been accepted back into the party, went on to succeed General Mulcahy as leader of Fine Gael in 1959.

Let us now look at the way the national desire to dismantle the Free State compromise of 1921–22 was reflected in the Galway general election poll in 1932:

Galway (City and County)   *9 seats*
Electorate 91,746. Quota 6,614.

3.	Frank Fahy, Fianna Fáil	6,132
1.	Thomas Powell, Fianna Fáil	6,068
2.	Patrick Hogan, Cumann na nGaedheal	5,551
	Mark Killilea, Fianna Fáil	5,454
5.	Patrick Beegan, Fianna Fáil	5,230
9.	Stephen Jordan, Fianna Fáil	5,142
	Frederick McDonogh, Cumann na nGaedheal	4,926
6.	Joseph William Mongan, Cumann na nGaedheal	4,926
7.	Seán Broderick, Cumann na nGaedheal	4,397
4.	Gerald Bartley, Fianna Fáil	4,357
	Seán Tubridy, Fianna Fáil	4,020
8.	Martin McDonogh, Cumann na nGaedheal	3,384
	Patrick Lambert, Cumann na nGaedheal	3,261
	Frank Kelly, Labour Party	1,533
	Edward J. Meehan, Labour Party	1,036
	Martin J. Cooke, Independent	987

Result: Fianna Fáil 5 (Bartley, Beegan, Fahy, Jordan and Powell). Cumann na nGaedheal 4 (Hogan, Mongan, Broderick and Mc-Donogh).

THERE WAS NO CHANGE IN the Cumann na nGaedheal line-out, except in the order of election, but in the case of Fianna Fáil obvious geographic and other alliances were already emerging within the party as the Fianna Fáil 'machine' became the most sophisticated operators of the complex PR system in western democracy. Two new names Paddy Beegan and Gerald Bartley are added to the list of 5 TDs that helped to bring Dev to power in 1932, and two outgoing TDs from the five elected in September 1927, Mark Killilea and Seán Tubridy, were not returned in spite of their impressive first preference votes in the 1932 poll. In the 'snap election' of January 1933 – the last time the old constituencies and the 153 seat total for the Dáil was used – there were further interesting developments.

Frank Fahy had been elected Ceann Comhairle, thereby guaranteeing Fianna Fáil one automatic seat, and reducing the choice from 9 seats (the largest constituency in the state since 1923) to 8 as far as voters were concerned.

1933 GENERAL ELECTION

Galway (City and County)   *9 seats*
Ceann Comhairle Frank Fahy returned automatically.
Electorate 94,591. Quota 8,105.

1.	Mark Killilea, Fianna Fáil	8,872
5.	Patrick Beegan, Fianna Fáil	7,010
4.	Gerald Bartley, Fianna Fáil	6,358
6.	Séamus P. Keely, Fianna Fáil	6,197
8.	Stephen Jordan, Fianna Fáil	5,770
	Thomas Powell, Fianna Fáil	5,687
	Seán Tubridy, Fianna Fáil	5,634
2.	Patrick Hogan, Cumann na nGaedheal	4,940
3.	Martin McDonogh, Cumann na nGaedheal	4,328
	Joseph Mongan, Cumann na nGaedheal	4,198
7.	Seán Broderick, Cumann na nGaedheal	4,167
	Frederick McDonogh, Cumann na nGaedheal	3,574
	Patrick Cawley, Cumann na nGaedheal	3,129
	Robert M. Burke, Labour Party	3,080

Result: Fianna Fáil 6 (Fahy, Killilea, Bartley, Beegan, Keely and Jordan, Fahy being automatically returned.)
Cumann na nGaedheal 3 (Hogan, Martin McDonogh and Broderick).

HAVING THE CEANN COMHAIRLE'S seat helped this strong Fianna Fáil performance. But the sophisticated use of geographic spread, and getting party loyalists to vote 'the full Republican ticket' are also obvious. The two former popular TDs, Thomas Powell and Seán Tubridy, were left sitting behind Stephen Jordan in the first preferences, and did not make it in the end. Instead Seamus Keely was elected, while Mark Killilea, IRA veteran and founding member of the party, who lost out in 1932, came back at the top of the poll, over the quota. Both Cumann na nGaedheal and Labour had gone into decline in Galway, probably because De Valera in office was articulating many of the radical social and economic policies that Labour should have been fighting for at that time. Within a year of this election clean sweep in Galway, Mark Killilea brought De Valera and Seán Lemass to his native Tuam to announce plans for the establishment of a state sugar factory, in the heart of Connacht, and Gerald Bartley announced Dev's first modest steps towards Gaeltacht reconstruction throughout Connemara in an attempt to dethrone Josie Mongan of Cumann na nGaedheal from his position as 'King of Connemara' in the 1920s, now that he had lost his seat.

It would be wrong to suggest that views of the Treaty and 1922 had changed very much. It is safer to venture the suggestion that the additional Fianna Fáil popularity in Galway derived mainly from the additional social and economic policies it put forward so effectively in the middle of a world depression. At the time it seemed to many that the Labour leadership was conservative and confused. 'We are the real Labour Party', Seán Lemass used to taunt in the Dáil and in terms of popular support he was probably correct. Nor should we forget the significant 'Republican card' which De Valera played, releasing political prisoners in 1932 that he would have back behind bars again within a few short years. It is a much neglected historical fact that the IRA (not Sinn Féin) worked privately but enthusiastically for Fianna Fáil in the elections in 1932, 1933 and the crucial 1934 local elections. But the impact of this is hard to quantify. Máirtín Ó Cadhain had considerable knowledge of this IRA support for De Valera in his early years in power.

Sinn Féin no longer contested Dáil elections, even in those areas where they had won seats in 1927. But IRA activists got out the hard-core Republican vote, against Cosgrave and for De Valera in 1932–33 even where in many cases Sinn Féin activists would normally opt for a boycott or spoilt vote. It should also be noted that the Galway electorate had declined to 94,591 in 1933 from 106,093 in 1923 when the first adult register of all males and females over 21 years was made available. These were tough economic times everywhere, and the measure of self-government which 26 counties gained at the beginning of the 1920s had not reflected any great increase in jobs in Galway or in most other Irish counties. The new Free State government had selected the university city of Galway as a focus for development in the west of Ireland. Ernest Blythe in particular defied his reputation as 'the minister for retrenchment' in Finance by decentralising or establishing various Irish-language schemes in Galway in the hope that a bilingual university, an Irish-speaking army battalion (an Chéad Chath), a state-sponsored Irish language theatre (an Taibhdhearc), not to mention a special salary bonus for gardaí who operated through Irish in the courts, would allow for the development of the national language as a normal urban language in the new Free State. But many had continued to emigrate due to poverty and lack of opportunities at home. The reality of the discrimination in Free State employment circles in the 1920s is one aspect of Cumann na nGaedheal corruption that is rarely, if ever, mentioned by historians. I will cite only one example concerning Seán Tubridy, a medical officer under the Galway Board of Health based in An Cheathrú Rua. He had been a medical officer with the Fourth Western Division of the IRA during the War of Independence, but he took the Republican side in the Civil War. For this, he was dismissed by sealed orders of the new Free State Department of Local Government in 1923. But he had to be reappointed 'for pragmatic reasons' as medical officer in Leitir Móir, in 1924 during a typhus epidemic. He was first elected in 1927 as a

Fianna Fáil TD. Things rallied somewhat under Dev in the 1930s, but it would take an economic war, a world war – The Emergency – and the financial policies of the post-war decade, before things started to improve in Galway.

Many of those who emigrated in the 1920s did so because the new native Irish government deprived even the most talented in their midst, of opportunities, and the right to earn their living, unless they signed up or swore true faith to the Free State, which clearly, even the political majority rejected as soon as they got the chance. The Free State was supported by many of its most enthusiastic backers, from Collins to Kevin O'Higgins to Mulcahy, Fitzgerald, Cosgrave and MacEoin, because, they argued, there was no other alternative. Ireland would have to use the 'Stepping Stone' which Britain had given, 'under the threat of immediate and terrible war'.

In the 1930s De Valera's Republican Party won two by-elections in Galway, when, on the death of Martin McDonogh, Fianna Fáil's Éamonn Corbett defeated Thomas McDonogh of Cumann na nGaedheal by 37,415 votes to 24,088 in the poll held on 19 June 1935. In the by-election arising from the death of Patrick Hogan, held on 13 August 1936, Martin Neilan (Fianna Fáil) was elected, but this time there was a Republican/Sinn Féin challenge to Dev, as the Blueshirt threat was receding, and relations between Fianna Fáil and the IRA – which played no small part in bringing Dev to power in 1932 – deteriorated rapidly after the first Republican martyr of the Fianna Fáil era, Seán Glynn of Limerick, died in custody. The full result of the 1936 by-election was: Martin Neilan, Fianna Fáil 39,982; James Hogan, Cumann na nGaedheal 23,264; George Nobel Count Plunkett, Sinn Féin 2,696.

By 1937 there were new constituencies, drawn up in 1935, to comply with the new electoral ratios, later outlined in Bunreacht na hÉireann. Total Dáil membership fell from 153 to 138 seats. Galway lost two seats and was divided into Galway East consisting of four seats and Galway West with three. Frank Fahy, the Ceann Comhairle, represented Galway East, thus effectively providing Fianna Fáil with three out of four seats in the East, and two out of three in Galway West.

Galway West   3 *seats*
Electorate 42,796. Quota 6,453.

1.	Seán Tubridy, Fianna Fáil,	7,274
2.	Gerald Bartley, Fianna Fáil	6,179
	Eamonn Corbett, Fianna Fáil	5,109
3.	Joseph William Mongan, Fine Gael	3,909
	Peter Kelly, Fine Gael	3,337

Result: Fianna Fáil 2 (Tubridy and Bartley) and Fine Gael 1, Joseph W. Mongan.

Galway East   4 *seats*
Electorate 49,476. Quota 8,474
Frank Fahy, Ceann Comhairle, automatically returned for Fianna Fáil.

2.	Mark Killilea, Fianna Fáil	8,067
1.	Patrick Beegan, Fianna Fáil	7,978
3.	Seán Broderick, Fine Gael	5,867
	Patrick Cawley, Fine Gael	4,275
	Stephen Jordan, Fianna Fáil	4,033
	Robert M. Burke, Labour	3,672

Result: Fianna Fáil 2 (Killilea and Beegan) and Frank Fahy, Ceann Comhairle. Fine Gael 1, Seán Broderick

IN 1938 THE SAME FOUR TDs were returned for East Galway but in a slightly different order. Electorate 48,530. Quota 8,758.

Frank Fahy, Ceann Comhairle, (1) was automatically returned for Fianna Fáil.

2.	Mark Killilea, Fianna Fáil	9,526
3.	Patrick Beegan, Fianna Fáil	8,804
4.	Seán Broderick, Fine Gael	6,339
	Patrick Cawley, Fine Gael	4,140
	Martin Regan, Fianna Fáil	3,468
	Robert M. Burke, Labour	2,753

Galway West   3 seats
Electorate 43,112. Quota 7,154.

1.	Gerald Bartley, Fianna Fáil	8,044
3.	Seán Tubridy, Fianna Fáil	6,346
	Louis E. O'Dea, Fianna Fáil	5,204
2.	Joseph W. Mongan, Fine Gael	4,172
	Peter Kelly, Fine Gael	2,803
	Michael O'Sullivan, Labour	2,046

Result: Fianna Fáil 2 (Bartley and Tubridy), Fine Gael 1, Mongan.

A CLEAR POLITICAL MOULD had been set down by this time in Galway which neither Michael Donnelan's Clann na Talmhan nor the death on hunger strike of Tony D'Arcy – a Headford IRA man who facilitated the first cumann meeting of Fianna Fáil in his area in 1929 – on 16 April 1940, could seriously disrupt. As far as West Galway (Connemara and the city) was concerned, it took the emergence of Peadar Mac an Iomaire, as a Gluaiseacht Chearta Sibhialta na Gaeltachta (non-party) candidate, in 1969, to challenge the 2–1 result in election after election in the three-seater. In 1969 Robert Molloy and Johnny Geoghegan were returned for Fianna Fáil and Fintan

Coogan took the Fine Gael third seat as had happened so often before. Still, Mac an Iomaire changed something in 1969 – and not just in the Gaeltacht either. It took an unlikely alliance of Fine Gael, Labour's Michael D. Higgins and two Sinn Féin/Republican Councillors to break the rigid monopoly of local power which Fianna Fáil had held on to, in Galway County Council from 1934, until they lost their overall majority after the 1979 local elections.

APPENDIX 1

BODIES OF EXECUTED REPUBLICANS RESTORED TO RELATIVES

A report from *The Westmeath Independent*, 1 November 1924:

On Tuesday the bodies of the 77 men executed during the year 1923 were handed over to their relatives by authority of the Adjutant General of the Saorstát military forces. They included those of Erskine Childers, Liam Mellows and Rory O'Connor, who were executed in Dublin.

At Dublin 18 bodies were handed over: at Tralee, 12: Dundalk, 5: Ennis, 3: Kilkenny, 2: Limerick, 2: Cork, 1: Athlone, 20: Curragh, 7: Roscrea, 3: Wexford, 3: Waterford, 2 and Carlow 1.

At Athlone the ceremony of handing over the remains commenced at 12 o'clock, the military chaplain officiating, Major-General McKeown, of the Western Command, and a number of staff officers, were also present. The remains were handed over to the friends at intervals of ten minutes each, and as each coffin passed out by the west gate, into the public square, military honours were rendered by the guard.

Notwithstanding the inclemency of the weather, a drenching downpour continuing from early morning, a large crowd had collected in the square, or market place, opposite the west gate of Custume Barracks. Many of the spectators were women and girls. Shortly after eleven o'clock, about twenty motor vehicles and a motor hearse arrived and were lined up from the Market Square, along the bridge to Custume Place. A few minutes before 12 o'clock, a guard of honour of IRA arrived, and was formed up in double line facing the entrance gate to the barracks. Some time later two soldiers carrying rifles, with bayonets fixed at the slope, emerged from the barracks and arrested a young man named Bernard

Mulvihill, who appeared to be in charge of the Republican guard of honour. He was conveyed into the barracks between the two soldiers, and as he passed in through the gates, a little cheer went up from the bystanders. The young man acknowledged the cheer by taking off his hat, after which there were shouts of 'Up the Republic'. Four other young men were arrested during the day. All five, who were searched for arms were subsequently set at liberty, no arms having being found on them.

The first body to be handed over was that of Michael Walsh, Derrymore, Caherlistrane, Co. Galway. He was executed at Athlone on January 20th, 1923. The body in addition to the coffin it was buried in originally, was encased in a large over sized oak coffin, stained yellow.

The coffins, containing the remains of Timothy O'Sullivan, William Street, Listowel; Charles Daly, Knockanescoulteen, Firies, Co. Kerry; John Larkin, Ballyharty, Magherafelt, Co. Derry; and Daniel Enright, Colbert Street, Listowel, Co. Kerry, were next handed over. These four young men were executed in Drumbo Castle, Tír Conaill, on March 14th, 1923. Their friends travelled from north and south the previous day, and arrived in Athlone on Monday night. Father Larkin, a brother of the executed Derryman, was also present at the receiving of the remains, as was also the brother of the late Charles Daly and a number of Kerrymen.

The others were handed over in the following order:

James O'Malley, Oughterard, Co. Galway; executed in Tuam, 11-4-'23.

Martin Moylan, Farmerstown, Annaghdown, Co. Galway; executed at Tuam on the same date.

John Maguire, Cross, Cong, Co. Mayo; executed Tuam, 11-4-'23.

Francis Cunnane, Kilconna, Headford, Co. Galway; executed at Tuam on the same date.

Michael Monaghan, Headford, Co. Galway; executed in Tuam on 11-4-'23.

Thomas Hughes, Boginfin, Athlone; executed at Athlone, January 20th, '23.

Stephen Joyce, Derrmore, Shrule, Co. Galway; executed Athlone on same date.

Hubert Collins, Headford, Co. Galway; executed Athlone, 20-1-'23.

Martin Burke, Shrule, Co. Galway; executed at Athlone, 20-1-'23.

John Newell, Headford, Co. Galway; executed at Tuam, 11-4-'23.

Patrick Cunningham, O'Connell Street, Tullamore; executed at Birr Castle on 26-1-'23.

Columb Kelly, Barrack Street, Tullamore.

Wm. Conroy, Clara Road, Tullamore; also executed at Birr Castle same date.

The bodies of the executed Kerrymen with that of Thomas Hughes, Boginfin were conveyed to Athlone Town Hall which had been prepared for their reception, and where they were deposited in the boardroom. A guard of honour was on duty at the hall all night. Temporary altars were erected in the room on which were placed lighted candles. The Rosary was recited for the souls of the dead when the coffins were placed in position alongside each other.

At 10 o'clock on Wednesday morning in the presence of a large crowd of spectators the coffins containing the remains of the dead Kerrymen were removed to waiting motor cars which conveyed them to their native places. Prayers for the dead were recited by Father O'Sullivan, brother of Timothy O'Sullivan, one of the deceased, before the removal of the coffins from the room.

The remains of the other executed men were brought to their respective homes on Tuesday evening. Each of the coffins was draped in the Republican Tricolour, and bore a breast-plate, provided by the relatives, on which was inscribed in Irish, the name, the date of death and age of the deceased.

The spectacle presented on Tuesday evening, after all the coffins had been removed from the barracks, was a never-to-be-forgotten-one, and a grim reminder of the unfortunate division between comrade Irishmen which was the result of Mr de Valera's refusal to accept the Treaty.* The long line of motor cars, intersected here and there by a huge yellow-painted coffin, formed indeed one of the most melancholy pictures ever witnessed in this or any other country.

*The figures given for the handing over of bodies at the various prisons and barracks are not entirely accurate. The clear editorial bias against De Valera, common in the media at that time, is also obvious at the end of this report

APPENDIX 2

TUAM WORKHOUSE

The Workhouse was opened on March 25th, 1846, but the Fever Hospital was not built for several years afterwards.

Although erected to accommodate 800, it is said that during the years 1846 and 1847 there were seldom less than 3,000 inmates (according to *Thom's [Directory]* there were 2,881 there in 1851).

During 1846 conditions in the town grew steadily worse. On October 5th the Town Commissioners were compelled to resolve that: 'Application be made to the Government for a sufficient military force under a Resident Magistrate to be stationed in Tuam for the purpose of securing the safe transit of goods and of affording protection to property, for the want of both which Tuam is, at present, in a deplorable state, and further, that Tuam be appointed a depot for provisions, in as much as that the town has been for the last three days, and still continues, without a supply of meal or flour, and that in consequence cattle have been taken off the streets and slaughtered by a starving populace.'

In 1847 cholera broke out and the epidemic, added to the already existing famine, had caused the year to be known as 'Black '47'. It is said that the roads around the town were dotted with the corpses of people who had died whilst trying to get to the town for food. In the absence of a fever hospital at the Workhouse, sheds were used to house the victims of the disease, and the old barracks were also requisitioned for the same purpose. A large pit was opened at Carrowpeter, in which, each evening, were buried those who had died during the day. When this pit had been filled with corpses another pit was opened at Ballymote. In 1947 the Old Tuam Society erected a stone monument to mark the site of the Carrowpeter burial ground, but there is no record of the number nor the identity of those buried there.

After the Famine the Workhouse continued to receive the home-less and the desolate. In 1916 came the Rising the subsequent war against the British Forces of Occupation. British Troops, among them the infamous Black and Tans, shifted the paupers out of the building and lodged themselves there. In the 1840s when all these Workhouses were built, the design always included the possibility that the building would be used as a Military Barracks, i.e., its defences were strong.

After the British left [in 1922] the Free State troops moved in and shortly afterwards on April 11th, 1923, six men, two groups of three were shot against the wall of the Oratory.

Source: *Eleven Galway Martyrs*, Tuam, 1985.

APPENDIX 3

UNVEILING CEREMONY 1985

The unveiling of the plaque on the memorial wall in Tuam on Sunday, 21 April 1985 was an impressive ceremony. Large crowds travelled from all the counties of the old First, Second, Third and Fourth Western Divisional areas, i.e., Galway itself, Clare, Mayo, Roscommon and Sligo. Groups came from as far away as Dublin and Cork, while Athlone was strongly represented

Following the parade to the old workhouse site from the 1916 memorial in Bishop Street, Cllr Frank Glynn of Milltown, former Chairman of Galway County Council, presided. He recalled that when the workhouse was built it was designed for easy conversion into a military stronghold, and was used as such by the British and later by the first Free State administration.

Describing the memorial wall, he pointed out that it was an unfinished pyramid. 'The pyramid will be completed only on the reunification and freedom of Ireland,' he said. He thanked the members of the Memorial Committee for their dedicated work for close on twenty years and all who assisted in such a noble project.

Peadar Hughes of Kilbeg led the gathering in the recitation of a decade of the Rosary in Irish. Many floral tributes were then laid. The Last Post and Reveille were sounded by bugler Robert Flynn of Castlerea as the crowd stood to attention.

The Proclamation of the Republic, Easter 1916 was read by Richard Behal of Killarney in the unavoidable absence of Joe Darcy, son of the late Comdt Tony Darcy. The Co. Galway Roll of Honour, listing casualties in the fight for Irish freedom from 1916 to the present day, was read by Murt Qualter of Athenry.

Comdt General Maguire inspected the colour-parties and the IRA Veterans lined up in front of the memorial. Following this he unveiled the plaque to loud and sustained applause and spoke briefly and feelingly of the deaths of the men of his command 62 years earlier.

Father Dominic Greally, Adm., Tuam blessed the memorial and recited a prayer specially composed for the occasion.

The oration was delivered by Ruairí Ó Brádaigh former TD who spoke first in Irish. In the course of his address he said:

'Today we stand on ground which is doubly sacred, for here British Imperial policy towards Ireland and the Irish people triumphed twice, if only temporarily. In the British enforced Great Starvation of our people in 1845, 1846 and 1847 thousands died on this very ground as part of a great holocaust of millions. They were buried without record in mass pits at Carrowpeter and Ballymote on the outskirts of this town, while food was exported from the country under armed escort of British soldiers. It was part of a policy of genocide against the Irish people for which the British establishment was never made amenable.

'Then in 1922–23 in carrying out the British policy of counter-revolution in 26 Irish counties, the Free State puppet regime executed as hostages our bravest and best on this very spot, surely a war-crime and a crime against humanity. There was no judicial Nuremburg Tribunal in Ireland; and Comdt Frank Cunnane in his last letter before facing the firing squad here asked that there be "no act of vengeance".

'In effect the Free Staters, at the bidding and with the support of England, brought off a *coup d'état* in the summer of 1922. They then presented the Irish people with a military "accomplished fact". The methods they used in this base and treacherous work are attested to by this memorial and many others like it throughout Ireland.

'The Irish people are entitled to their historic demand, a free and united country. They are also entitled as a sovereign people to neutrality and non-alignment. One demand cannot be traded off against the other and we should resist all efforts to trap us into a military alliance of whatever description.

'The late Ernie O'Malley, great fighter for Irish freedom, wrote in his book *On Another Man's Wound* of the idealism, courage and spirit of no compromise that motivated so many Irish people following the 1916 Rising. He penned these evocative lines to express that feeling for Ireland, for the Holy Grail of the Republic: "The blood sang and pulsed. A strange love was born that for some was never to die till they lay stiff on the hillside or in quicklime near a barrack wall." How true this was of the soldiers who gave their all here and in Athlone.

'Ernie O'Malley dedicated his book 'To Ireland, the Ever-Living and her Dead Sons'. I wish to dedicate this memorial similarly, but also to her Dead Daughters for none were more loyal. May it stand here as an eternal reproach to any and all who would delay by one day – or even one hour – the final and fullest realisation of the ideals for which our Republican soldiers died!'

GENERAL MAGUIRE'S ADDRESS

Having unveiled the memorial plaque, Comdt Gen. Tom Maguire [92] addressed the crowd briefly:

'It is an honour and a privilege to unveil this plaque. The Republican soldiers who died here and their comrades in Athlone fell before Free State firing squads. They were all attached to the Second Western Division which I commanded. They were my men and their blood was spilt by those who were unfit. They gave their lives for the All-Ireland Republic then under attack. That Republic was overthrown and has yet to be restored.

'They were my men,' General Maguire repeated, 'and they were faithful. They were faithful to their oath to defend the Republic against all enemies, foreign and domestic. Others were unfaithful, were unworthy.

'Pádraig Pearse, first President of the All-Ireland Republic in 1916, wrote a poem dedicated to his mother while in his death cell awaiting execution. In it his mother speaks of her two sons and says: "My sons were faithful and they fought". This was indeed true of the men who died here and in Athlone and all over Ireland in a similar manner at that time. It is good that their sacrifices are commemorated, but we must also remember that their objective remains unattained.

'I wish to thank the Tuam Memorial Committee for calling on me to carry out this task. I am proud to be associated with today's worthy ceremony.'

Source: *Eleven Galway Martyrs*, Tuam, 1985.

APPENDIX 4

COMDT GENERAL TOM MAGUIRE, GOC
SECOND WESTERN DIVISION IRA
and TD for South Mayo–South Roscommon from 1921 to 1927 looks
back on the Civil War in Connacht, 60 years later

Cmdt General Tom Maguire spoke to Uinseann MacEoin, editor of the book Survivors
(1980) about the Civil War – also called the Second Defence of the Republic – in his area
(Reprinted by kind permission of Uinseann MacEoin).

THERE HAD BEEN NO military confrontations in this part of the west.
The British evacuated Ballinrobe, Claremorris and other towns
and we were in control. We heard of the attack upon the Four
Courts from the newspapers. The position here was that there was
no strong force opposing us. However, here, as everywhere else,
we adopted the strategy of evacuation. We had not the material, so
we retired from the barracks and made for the hills. There was no
cohesion or military council formed between the provincial commanders here, Liam Pilkington of the Third Western, Mick Kilroy
of the Fourth or myself. There were instead many desertions; you
might be in touch with personalities on your side today, and
tomorrow you could be told that they had gone over to the Free
State. (The rapid and businesslike way whereby the Free State
gained control of the country, especially in areas where Republican garrisons were undecided was a major factor in this.) It had a
weakening effect upon our effort.

I was back upon the run again, mainly in South Mayo. I was
concerned very much by what you termed fragmentation, by the
effort to travel around, make contact, and hold our groups together. Ours was a wholly defensive strategy. While we made a few
attacks upon Free State posts, I can think of nothing spectacular,
certainly there was no longer the thinking or the will-power that
had created the ambushes of a year and a half ago.

You could not bring yourself to want this sort of warfare. There was a different feeling altogether. The British were the enemy, the old enemy: there was a certain pride in having the ability to attack them. That feeling was entirely absent in the Civil War. It was very disheartening. We knew the Free State army comprising 50,000 newly recruited mercenaries would not hesitate to shoot us, but that made it no easier for us to pluck up enough anger to really fight them. You were in doubt too about approaching houses where before you had been made welcome. How are they taking the situation, you would wonder? The people themselves were disheartened.

When I heard of the deaths of people on the Free State side like Griffith, Collins and Seán Hales, I could not be glad. You felt these are people who fought the British and now they are gone. Britain is really the victor.

It was on October 10th [1922] they passed the Army Powers Resolution, the Murder Act, as we called it, giving tribunals power to execute anyone found carrying arms or ammunition, aiding or abetting in attacks, destruction or seizure of property; so wide indeed was it, that it could be used against anyone having any connection with the Republican resistance. The implementation of such draconian powers enraged us but it was futile. We could make no response in the circumstances. I was captured myself anyway just a few days after that in the Headford district. I was at my usual task of getting around, trying to hold things together. Suddenly a body of Free State soldiers were in on top of me and I was captured. It was then that I really experienced the sort of mercenaries they were, ex-British army soldiers, tramps and misfits of every conceivable type. They had expanded their army to over 50,000 men and I suppose you do not find numbers like that unless you rake them from off the street corners.

I was brought to Athlone where there were two prison camps within the boundaries of the former British army military barracks.

In one, known as Pump Square, they held the ordinary detainees and prisoners. In the other, Garrison Detention, they kept people arrested after the passing of the Murder Act. There were regular cells in the Detention, and it was well enclosed as it had been used to hold the delinquents of the British army. Having been caught in arms after the passing of the Resolution I was held there, from October 1922 until June 1923, when I escaped out of it. During all the months I was there I never knew but that I might be executed. Five men were shot there by a firing squad in January, my youngest brother John, not yet twenty years of age, was executed in Tuam, only forty miles away in April 1923. It seems like, from the way Peadar O'Donnell tells in a book of his, they found it easier to make an example of younger brothers, leaving the older and more senior ones alone. I was a TD, but that had not saved Mellows or Childers, and I did not expect that it would save me.'*

THE SIXTH MAN

They courtmartialled me in January 1923. The court, if you could call it that, was a military one although they were all in civies. I enquired when I was brought in 'what is this?' although I knew damned well. 'I do not recognise this court,' I answered, 'you have no authority to try me.' They went through their rigmarole of accusations nonetheless, and of course they found me guilty. The day before, the five executions I have just spoken about, a military policeman of theirs, a Segt Browne came in and handed a list of six names to Dr Tom Powell, our OC. Powell came to me. 'This fellow says that he has instructions to take these people from their ordinary cells tonight and put them into different cells.' The six men were changed that night before lock-up: five were taken out in the morning and shot by firing squad, and one was not. I am that one. I often thought afterwards how did that happen to me, but I can-

* However both Childers and Mellows lost their Dáil seats in the June 1922 (Pact) election, while Maguire was returned again as TDÉ [Teachta Dála Éireann] for South Mayo/South Roscommon.

not tell you. Unless it was because I was popular, I did have a reputation for fair play. During the Tan struggle unionists and loyalists could call upon me if someone was trying to lean upon them.

... It is said that the Free State 'provincialised' its killings, both official and unofficial, by having the majority of them carried out away from Dublin in contrast to the British who had all of theirs, except one, in Dublin and Cork. It is my opinion that their objective was to involve all of their senior officers in this policy, so that there would be no denying it afterwards. Joe Sweeney carried out executions in Drumboe in Donegal. Dan Hogan had them in Dundalk. Michael McCormick had them in Portlaoise, Birr and Roscrea, Joseph Cummins had them in Wexford, Liam Stack had one in Carlow, Seán MacEoin had them in Athlone and Michael Brennan had them in Tuam, Limerick and Ennis. Eleven of my command were executed by them. With my brother, John, five others were executed in Tuam on April 11th. (The executions of March, April & May 1923 were unnecessarily vengeful: the Free Staters knew that the IRA was about to suspend its resistance.) He had been arrested in the Tuam area sometime after myself and they had far less on him.

APPENDIX 5

EXECUTED REPUBLICANS

1916

(Sixteen Men)

P. H. Pearse, shot in Dublin, 3 May
Tom Clarke, shot in Dublin, 3 May
Thomas McDonagh, shot in Dublin, 3 May
Joseph Plunkett, shot in Dublin, 4 May
Edward Daly, shot in Dublin, 4 May
William Pearse, shot in Dublin, 4 May
Michael O'Hanrahan, shot in Dublin, 4 May
John MacBride, shot in Dublin, 5 May
Eamon Ceannt, shot in Dublin, 8 May
Michael Mallin, shot in Dublin, 8 May
Con Colbert, shot in Dublin, 8 May
Seán Heuston, shot in Dublin, 8 May
Thomas Kent, shot in Cork, 9 May
Seán MacDermott, shot in Dublin, 12 May
James Connolly, shot in Dublin, 12 May
Roger Casement, hanged in Pentonville Prison (London), 3 August

1920–21

(Twenty-four Men)

Kevin Barry, hanged in Dublin, 1 November 1920*
Cornelius Murphy, shot in Cork, 1 February 1921
Thomas O'Brien, shot in Cork, 28 February 1921
Daniel O'Callaghan, shot in Cork, 28 February 1921
John Lyons, shot in Cork, 28 February 1921
Timothy McCarthy, shot in Cork, 28 February 1921
Patrick O'Mahony, shot in Cork, 28 February 1921
John Allen, shot in Cork, 28 February 1921

Thomas Whelan, hanged in Dublin, 14 March 1921

Patrick Moran, hanged in Dublin, 14 March 1921

Thomas Bryan, hanged in Dublin, 14 March 1921.

Patrick Doyle, hanged in Dublin, 14 March 1921

Frank Flood, hanged in Dublin, 14 March 1921

Bernard Ryan, hanged in Dublin, 14 March 1921

Thomas Traynor, hanged in Dublin, 26 April 1921

Patrick Sullivan, shot in Cork, 28 April 1921

Maurice Moore, shot in Cork, 28 April 1921

Patrick Ronayne, shot in Cork, 28 April 1921

Thomas Mulcahy, shot in Cork, 28 April 1921

Patrick Casey, shot in Cork, 2 May 1921

Daniel O'Brien, shot in Cork, 16 May 1921

Thomas Keane, shot in Limerick, 4 June 1921

Edward Foley, hanged in Dublin, 7 June 1921

Patrick Maher, hanged in Dublin, 7 June 1921

During the Black and Tan War Volunteers were hanged in Dublin but shot in Cork and Limerick following the imposition of martial law in the south. Kevin Barry was the first executed martyr by hanging of the War of Independence era. Connaught Ranger mutineer Jim Daly was shot in India the following day, 2 November 1920.

1922–23
(Seventy-seven Men)

The following were executed by shooting:
James Fisher, in Dublin, 17 November 1922

Peter Cassidy, in Dublin, 17 November 1922

Richard Twohig, in Dublin, 17 November 1922

J. Gaffney, in Dublin, 17 November 1922

Erskine Childers, in Dublin, 24 November 1922

Jos. Spooner, in Dublin, 30 November 1922

Patrick Farrelly, in Dublin, 30 November 192.

John Murphy, in Dublin, 30 November 1922

Rory O'Connor, in Dublin, 8 December 1922

Liam Mellows, in Dublin, 8 December 1922

Joseph McKelvey, in Dublin, 8 December 1922

Richard Barrett, in Dublin, 8 December 1922

Stephen White, in Dublin, 19 December 1922
Joseph Johnston, in Dublin, 19 December 1922
Patrick Mangan, in Dublin, 19 December 1922
Patrick Nolan, in Dublin, 19 December 1922
Brian Moore, in Dublin, 19 December 1922
James O'Connor, in Dublin, 19 December 1922
Patrick Bagnel, in Dublin, 19 December 1922
John Phelan, in Kilkenny, 29 December 1922
John Murphy, in Kilkenny, 29 December 1922
Leo Dowling, in Dublin, 8 January 1923
Sylvester Heaney, in Dublin, 8 January 1923
Laurence Sheehy, in Dublin, 8 January 1923
Anthony O'Reilly, in Dublin, 8 January 1923
Terence Brady, in Dublin, 8 January 1923
Thomas McKeown, in Dundalk, 13 January 1923
John McNulty, in Dundalk, 13 January 1923
Thomas Murray, in Dundalk, 13 January 1923
F. Burke, in Roscrea, 15 January 1923
Patrick Russell, in Roscrea, 15 January 1923
Martin O'Shea, in Roscrea 15 January 1923
Patrick MacNamara, in Roscrea, 15 January 1923
James Lillis, in Carlow, 15 January 1923
James Daly, in Tralee, 20 January 1923
John Clifford, in Tralee, 20 January 1923
Michael Brosnan, in Tralee, 20 January 1923
James Hanlon, in Tralee, 20 January 1923
Cornelius McMahon, in Limerick, 20 January 1923
Patrick Hennessy, in Limerick, 20 January 1923
Thomas Hughes, in Athlone, 20 January 1923
Michael Walsh, in Athlone, 20 January 1923
Hubert Collins, in Athlone, 20 January 1923
Stephen Joyce, in Athlone, 20 January 1923
Martin Burke, in Athlone, 20 January 1923
James Melia, in Dundalk, 22 January 1923
Thomas Lennon, in Dundalk, 22 January 1923
Joseph Ferguson, in Dundalk, 22 January 1923
Michael Fitzgerald, in Waterford, 25 January 1923
Patrick O'Reilly, in Waterford, 25 January 1923
Patrick Cunningham, in Birr, 26 January 1923

William Conroy, in Birr, 26 January 1923
Colum Kelly, in Birr, 26 January 1923
Patrick Geraghty, in Port Laoise, 27 January 1923
Joseph Byrne, in Port Laoise, 27 January 1923
Thomas Gibson, in Port Laoise, 26 February 1923
James O'Rourke, in Dublin, 13 March 1923
William Healy, in Cork, 13 March 1923
James Pearle, in Wexford, 13 March 1923
Patrick Hogan, in Wexford, 13 March 1923
John Creane, in Wexford, 13 March 1923
Tim O'Sullivan, in Drumboe, 14 March 1923
Charles Daly, in Drumboe, 14 March 1923
John Larkin, in Drumboe, 14 March 1923
Dan Enright, in Drumboe, 14 March 1923
Séamus O'Malley, in Tuam, 11 April 1923
Frank Cunnane, in Tuam, 11 April 1923
Michael Monaghan, in Tuam, 11 April 1923
Seán Newell, in Tuam, 11 April 1923
Seán Maguire, in Tuam, 11 April 1923
Martin Moylan, in Tuam, 11 April 1923
Edward Greaney, in Tralee, 25 April 1923
Reginald Hathaway, in Tralee, 25 April 1923
James McInerney, in Tralee, 25 April 1923
Patrick Mahoney, in Ennis, 26 April 1923
Chris Quinn, in Ennis, 2 May 1923
William Shaughnessy, in Ennis, 2 May 1923

APPENDIX 6

ELECTION RESULTS 1918–23

1. General Election, December 1918

Number of seats in the whole of Ireland	105
Returned: SINN FÉIN	73
NATIONALISTS (Supporters of the Parliamentary Party)	6
4 were returned by agreement with Sinn Féin	
UNIONISTS, 23 were returned in north-east Ulster	26

2. Municipal Elections, January 1920

Number of Corporations and Councils in Ireland	127
Number to which a Republican majority was elected	72
Number to which a majority of Republicans and	
Nationalists were returned by agreed voting	26
Number to which a majority of Unionists was elected	29

*3. Elections for County and Rural Districts Councils and
Boards of Poor Law Guardians, June 1920*

Number of County Councils in Ireland	33
Number to which a Republican majority was elected	28
Number of Rural Councils in Ireland	206
Number to which a Republican majority was elected	182
Number of Poor Law Boards in Ireland	154
Number to which a Republican majority was elected	138

4. Elections, May 1921 ('The Partition Elections')

Number of seats in 'Southern Ireland' (Twenty-six counties)	128
Returned: SINN FÉIN	124
UNIONISTS	4

Number of seats in 'Northern Ireland' (Six counties)	52
Returned: UNIONISTS	40
SINN FÉIN	6
NATIONALISTS	6

5. General Election, Twenty-six counties area only, June 1922 ('The Pact Election')

Number of seats in the Twenty-six counties	128
Returned: PRO-TREATY CANDIDATES	58
REPUBLICANS [ANTI-TREATY]	36
LABOUR	17
FARMERS	7
INDEPENDENTS	10

6. General Election, Irish Free State, August 1923

Number of seats	153
Returned: CUMANN NA NGAEDHEAl (Pro-Treaty)	63
REPUBLICANS	44
FARMERS	15
LABOUR	14
INDEPENDENTS	17

* * * *

'The government had the usual support of the press and strong backing from the other pro-Treaty elements. Sinn Féin suffered continual harassment and disruption, with most of its candidates interned or on the run. (As a result, women and youth played the major part in electioneering.) In view of its apparent advantages, the result came as an unpleasant shock for the government. They had won the largest number of seats, 63, but Sinn Féin won 44 – more than twice their best hopes ...

'There had been signs during the campaign that the Free State government was not having it all its own way. Reports told how William Cosgrave raged over his reception in what was supposed to be a friendly area – being unable to hire the local bands, an un-welcome guest at a hurling match, and then finding a memorial card for Liam Mellows and Erskine Childers under his plate at an official dinner ... in County Kerry black-shawled mothers knelt in the streets and cursed him for the murder of their sons.'

Source: *The Irish Civil War 1922–1923*, Frances M. Blake, London 1986

APPENDIX 7

MANIFESTO OF THE IRISH VOLUNTEERS*

At a time when legislative proposals, universally confessed to be of vital concern for the future of Ireland, have been put forward, and are awaiting decision, a plan has been deliberately adopted by one of the great English political parties, advocated by the leaders of that party and by its numerous organs in the press, and brought systematically to bear on English public opinion, to make a display of military force and the menace of armed violence the determining factor in the future relations between this country and Great Britain.

The party which has thus substituted open force for the semblance of civil government is seeking by this means not merely to decide an immediately political issue of grave concern to this Nation, but also to obtain for itself the future control of all our national affairs. It is plain to every man that the people of Ireland, if they acquiesce in this new policy by their inaction will consent to the surrender not only of their rights as a nation, but of their civic rights as men.

The Act of Union deprived the Irish nation of the power to direct its own course and to develop and use its own resources for its own benefit. It gave us instead the meagre and seldom effective right of throwing our votes into the vast and complicated movement of British politics. Since the Act of Union, a long series of representative statutes has endeavoured to deal with the incessant discontent of the Irish people by depriving them of various rights common to all who live under the British Constitution.

The new policy goes further than the Act of Union, and further than all subsequent Coercion Acts taken together. It proposes to leave us the political franchise in name and to annihilate it in fact. If we fail to take such measures as will effectually defeat this policy, we become politically the most degraded population in Europe, and no longer worthy of the name of Nation.

Are we to rest inactive in the hope that the course of politics in Great Britain may save us from the degradation openly threatened against us? British politics are controlled by British interests, and are complicated by problems of great importance to the people of Great Britain. In a crisis of this kind the duty of safe-guarding our rights is our duty first and foremost. If we remain quiescent by what title can we expect the people of Great Britain to turn aside from their own pressing concerns to defend us? Will not such an attitude of itself mark us out as a people unworthy of defence?

Such is the occasion, not altogether unfortunate, which has brought about the inception of the Irish Volunteer movement. But the Volunteers, once they have been enrolled, will form a prominent element in the national life under a National Government. The nation will maintain its Volunteer organisation as a guarantee of the liberties which the Irish people shall have secured.

If ever in history a people could say that an opportunity was given them by God's will to make an honest and manly stand for their rights, that opportunity is given us today. The stress of industrial efforts, the relative peace and prosperity of recent years, may have dulled the sense of the full demands of civic duty. We may forget that the powers of the platform, the press and the polling booth are derived from the conscious resolve of the people to maintain their rights and liberties. From time immemorial it has been held by every race of mankind to be the right and duty of a freeman to defend his freedom with all his resources and with his life itself. The exercise of that right distinguishes the freeman from the serf, the discharge of that duty distinguishes him from the coward.

To drill, to learn the use of arms, to acquire the habit of concerted and disciplined action, to form a citizen army from a population now at the mercy of almost any organised aggression – this, beyond all doubt, is a programme that appeals to all Ireland, but especially to young Ireland. We begin at once in Dublin, and we are confident that the movement will be taken up without delay all over the country. Public opinion has already and quite spontaneously formed itself into an eager desire for the establishment of the Irish Volunteers.

The object proposed for the Irish Volunteers is to secure and maintain the rights and liberties common to all the people of Ireland. Their duties will be defensive and protective, and they will not contemplate either aggression or domination. Their ranks are open to all able-bodied Irishmen without distinction of creed, politics, or social grade. Means will be found whereby Irishmen unable to serve as ordinary Volunteers will be enabled to aid the Volunteer forces in various capacities. There will also be work for women to do, and there are signs that the women of Ireland, true to their record, are especially enthusiastic for the success of the Irish Volunteers.

We propose for the Volunteers' organisation the widest possible basis. Without any other association or classification the Volunteers will be enrolled according to the district in which they live. As soon as it is found feasible, the district sections will be called upon to join in making provision for the general administration and discipline and for united co-operation. The Provisional Committee which has acted up to the present will continue to offer its services until an elective body is formed to replace it.

A proportion of time spared, not from work, but from pleasure and recreation, a voluntary adoption of discipline, a purpose firmly and steadily carried through, will renew the vitality of the nation. Even that degree of self-discipline will bring back to every town, village and countryside a consciousness that has long been forbidden them – the sense of freemen who have fitted themselves to defend the cause of freedom.

In the name of National unity, of National dignity, of National and individual Liberty, of manly citizenship, we appeal to our countrymen to recognise and accept without hesitation the opportunity that has been granted them to join the ranks of the Irish Volunteers, and to make the movement now begun not unworthy of the historic title which it has adopted.

* Read at their Inaugural Meeting in Dublin, 25 November 1913

APPENDIX 8

ADDRESS OF IRISH COMMANDANTS
TO THE PRESIDENT AND CONGRESS OF THE UNITED STATES

[The following address was drafted on 18 June 1917, by Republican Commandants who arrived on that day from England, where they had been prisoners since 1916. It was brought to the United States by Dr Patrick McCartan and publicly received at the Capital by Secretary Tumulty.]

Dublin, Ireland, June 18, 1917

Gentlemen:

We, the undersigned, who have been held in English prisons and have been dragged from dungeon to dungeon, in heavy chains, cut off, since Easter Week, 1916, from all intercourse with the outside world, have just had an opportunity of seeing the printed text of the message of the United States of America to the Provisional Government of Russia.

We see that the President accepts as the aim of both countries 'the carrying of the present struggle for the freedom of all peoples to a successful consummation.' We, also, see that the object of President Wilson's own government is 'the liberation of peoples everywhere from the aggressions of autocratic force.' 'We are fighting,' writes the President to the Government of Russia, 'for the liberty, self-government, and undictated development of all peoples, and every feature of the settlement that concludes this war must be conceived and executed for that purpose. Wrongs must first be righted, and then adequate safeguards must be created to prevent their being committed again. Remedies must be found as well as statements of principle that will have a pleasing and sonorous sound ... No people must be forced under a sovereignty under which it does not wish to live.'

We trust that such remedies – in preference to any governmental professions whatsoever – will be held to include the right of each people, not merely to rely on other peoples to support their claim to national liberty, but what the Governments and people of other nations will, we trust, regard as even more sacred, the right of each people to defend itself against external aggression, external interference and external control. It is this particular right that we claim for the Irish people, and not content with statements of principle, though these themselves may be made a pretext for our oppression, we are engaged and mean to engage ourselves in practical means for establishing this right.

Without awaiting the issue of the war or the settlement that may conclude the war, we ask of the Government of the United States of America, and the Governments of the free peoples of the world, to take immediate measure to inform themselves accurately and on the spot about the extent of liberty or attempted repression which we may encounter.

We, the undersigned, are officers (just released from English prisons) of forces formed independently in Ireland to secure the complete liberation of the Irish Nation.

(Signed)

Éamon de Valéra

Eóin MacNéill

Donnchadh Ua Ceallacháin

Séamus Ua Laoidhléis

Riobard Ó Breandain

M. D. De Lásaigh

Fionán Ó Loinsigh

Proinnsias Ó Fathaigh

Tomás Ua Fiadhachra

Séan R. Etchingham

Risteard Mac Conríogh

Séan Mac an tSaoi

Risteard Ó hAodha

Séumas Doyle

Peadar Galligan

Tomás Ághas

Diarmuid Ua Loinsigh

Risteard Ó Colmáin

Seóirse Ó h-Éireamhóin

Conchubhar Ó Coileáin

Aoibhistin de Staic

Séan Mac Gadhra

T. Deasmhumhan Mac Gearailt

Proinnsías Ó Droighneáin

Frainc Ó Laoidhléis

Séamus S. Breathnach

APPENDIX 9

THE CONSTITUTION OF SINN FÉIN*

I

1. The name of this organisation shall be Sinn Féin.

2. Sinn Féin aims at securing the International recognition of Ireland as an independent Irish Republic.

Having achieved that status the Irish people may by referendum freely choose their own form of Government.

3. This object shall be attained through the Sinn Féin Organisation.

4. WHEREAS no law made without the authority and consent of the Irish people is or ever can be binding on their conscience

> Therefore in accordance with the Resolution of Sinn Féin adopted in Convention, 1905, a Constituent Assembly shall be convoked, comprising persons chosen by the Irish Constituencies as the supreme national authority to speak and act in the name of the Irish people and to devise and formulate measures for the welfare of the whole people of Ireland.

Such as:

(a) The introduction of a Protective System for Irish industries and Commerce by combined action of the Irish County Councils, Urban Councils, Rural Councils, Poor Law Boards, Harbour Boards, and other bodies directly responsible to the Irish people.

(b) The establishment and maintenance under the direction of a National Assembly or other authority approved by the people of Ireland of an Irish Consular Service for the advancement of Irish Commerce and Irish interests generally.

(c) The re-establishment of an Irish Mercantile Marine to facilitate direct trading between Ireland and the countries of Continental Europe, America, Africa and the Far East.

(d) The industrial survey of Ireland and the development of its mineral resources under the auspices of a National Assembly or other national authority approved by the people of Ireland.

(e) The establishment of a National Stock Exchange.

(f) The creation of a National Civil Service, embracing all the employees of the County Councils, Rural Councils, Poor Law Boards, Harbour Boards and other bodies responsible to the Irish people, by the institution of a common national qualifying examination and a local competitive examination (the latter at the discretion of the local bodies).

(g) The establishment of Sinn Féin Courts of Arbitration for the speedy and satisfactory adjustment of disputes.

(h) The development of transit by rail, road and water, of waste lands for the national benefit by a National Authority approved by the people of Ireland.

(i) The development of the Irish Sea Fisheries by National Assembly or other National Authority approved by the people of Ireland.

(j) The reform of education, to render its basis national and industrial by the compulsory teaching of the Irish language, Irish history and Irish agricultural and manufacturing potentialities in the primary system, and, in addition, to elevate to a position of dominance in the university system Irish agriculture and economics.

(k) The abolition of the Poor Law System and substitution in its stead of adequate outdoor relief to the aged and infirm, and the employment of the able-bodied in the reclamation of waste lands, afforestation and other national and reproductive works.

II

A Special meeting of the Executive may be summoned on three days' notice by the President on requisition presented to him signed by six members of the Executive specifying the object for which the meeting is called.

In case of an urgent emergency the President shall call all members of the Executive to an urgency meeting, and may take action in the name of the Executive in case he secures the approval of an absolute majority of the entire Executive. The action taken is to be reported for confirmation at next ordinary meeting of the Executive.

III

That where Irish resources are being developed, or where industries exist, Sinn Féiners should make it their business to secure that workers are paid a living wage.

That the equality of men and women in this Organisation be emphasised in all speeches and leaflets.

* As adopted by the Árdfheis which met in Dublin on 25 October 1917.

APPENDIX 10

MANIFESTO OF SINN FÉIN*

The coming general election is fraught with vital possibilities for the future of our nation. Ireland is faced with the question whether this generation wills it that she is to march out into the full sunlight of freedom, or is to remain in the shadow of a base imperialism that has brought and ever will bring in its train naught but evil for our race.

Sinn Féin gives Ireland the opportunity of vindicating her honour and pursuing with renewed confidence the path of national salvation by rallying to the flag of the Irish Republic.

Sinn Féin aims at securing the establishment of that Republic:

1. By withdrawing the Irish Representation from the British Parliament and by denying the right and opposing the will of the British government or any other foreign government to legislate for Ireland.

2. By making use of any and every means available to render impotent the power of England to hold Ireland in subjection by military force or otherwise.

3. By the establishment of a constituent assembly comprising persons chosen by Irish constituencies as the supreme national authority to speak and act in the name of the Irish people, and to develop Ireland's social, political and industrial life, for the welfare of the whole people of Ireland.

4. By appealing to the Peace Conference for the establishment of Ireland as an Independent Nation. At that conference the future of the Nations of the world will be settled on the principle of government by consent. Ireland's claim to the application of that principle in her favour is not based on any accidental situation arising from the war. It is older than many if not all of the present belligerents. It is based on our unbroken tradition of nationhood, on a unity in

a national name which has never been challenged, on our possession of a distinctive national culture and social order, on the moral
courage and dignity of our people in the face of alien aggression,
on the fact that in nearly every generation, and five times within
the past 120 years our people have challenged in arms the right of
England to rule this country. On these incontrovertible facts is
based the claim that our people have beyond question established
the right to be accorded all the power of a free nation.

Sinn Féin stands less for a political party than for the Nation;
it represents the old tradition of nationhood handed on from dead
generations; it stands by the Proclamation of the Provisional Government of Easter, 1916, reasserting the inalienable right of the Irish
Nation to sovereign independence, reaffirming the determination
of the Irish people to achieve it, and guaranteeing within the independent Nation equal rights and equal opportunities to all its
citizens.

Believing that the time has arrived when Ireland's voice for
the principle of untrammelled National self-determination should
be heard above every interest of party or class, Sinn Féin will op-
pose at the polls every individual candidate who does not accept
this principle.

The policy of our opponents stands condemned on any test,
whether of principle or expediency. The right of a nation to sovereign independence rests upon immutable natural law and cannot be made the subject of a compromise. Any attempt to barter
away the sacred and inviolate rights of nationhood begins in dis-
honour and is bound to end in disaster. The enforced exodus of
millions of our people, the decay of our industrial life, the ever-
increasing financial plunder of our country, the whittling down of
the demand for the 'Repeal of the Union,' voiced by the first Irish
Leader to plead in the Hall of the Conqueror to that of Home Rule
on the Statute Book, and finally the contemplated mutilation of our
country by partition, are some of the ghastly results of a policy that

leads to national ruin.

Those who have endeavoured to harness the people of Ireland to England's war-chariot, ignoring the fact that only a freely-elected government in a free Ireland has power to decide for Ireland the question of peace and war, have forfeited the right to speak for the Irish people. The green flag turned red in the hands of the leaders, but that shame is not to be laid at the doors of the Irish people unless they continue a policy of sending their representatives to an alien and hostile assembly, whose powerful influence has been sufficient to destroy the integrity and sap the independence of their representatives. Ireland must repudiate the men who, in a supreme crisis for the nation, attempted to sell her birthright for the vague promises of English ministers, and who showed their incompetence by failing to have even these promises fulfilled.

The present Irish members of the English parliament constitute an obstacle to be removed from the path that leads to the Peace Conference. By declaring their will to accept the status of a province instead of boldly taking their stand upon the right of the nation they supply England with the only subterfuge at her disposal for obscuring the issue in the eyes of the world. By their persistent endeavours to induce the young manhood of Ireland to don the uniform of our seven-century old oppressor, and place their lives at the disposal of the military machine that holds our Nation in bondage they endeavour to barter away and even to use against itself the one great asset still left to our Nation after the havoc of centuries.

Sinn Féin goes to the polls handicapped by all the arts and contrivances that a powerful and unscrupulous enemy can use against us. Conscious of the power of Sinn Féin to secure the freedom of Ireland the British government would destroy it. Sinn Féin, however, goes to the polls confident that the people of this ancient nation will be true to the old cause and will vote for the men who stand by the principles of Tone, Emmet, Mitchel, Pearse and Connolly, the men who disdain to whine to the enemy for favours, the men who hold that Ireland must be as free as England or Holland, or Switzerland or France, and whose demand is that the only status befitting this ancient realm is the status of a free nation.

Prepared for the general election of December 1918 but dramatically censored by Dublin Castle.

APPENDIX 11

INVITATION
TO THE ELECTED REPRESENTATIVES OF THE IRISH PEOPLE, 7 JANUARY 1919

6 Sráid Fhearchair,
Áth Cliath.
8.1.19

A Chara,

At a meeting held in the Mansion House on the 7th inst. of the Republican representatives of Ireland, elected at the General Election of 1918, the following resolutions were adopted:

(1) 'That we, the Republican members of the Irish constituencies, in accordance with the National Will, are empowered to call together the Dáil Éireann, and proceed to act accordingly.'

(2) 'That all persons elected by the existing Irish constituencies as members of Parliament at the General Election of December, 1918, be invited to attend as members of the Dáil Éireann as an independent Constituent Assembly of the Irish Nation.'

In accordance with the following resolutions, I have the honour of inviting you to attend the opening of An Dáil Éireann, which will be held in Dublin at an early date.

I shall be glad to have a reply from you at your earliest convenience.

Mise,
G. N. COUNT PLUNKETT
Chairman of meeting of Republican Representatives

Appendix 12

Constitution of Dáil Éireann*

First Section

 Dáil Éireann shall possess full powers to legislate and shall be composed of Delegates (Teachtaí) chosen by the people of Ireland from the present constituencies of the country.

Second Section

 (1) Full executive powers shall be held at any time by the Ministry (Aireacht) in office at the time.

 (2) The Ministry shall be composed of the following: A Prime Minister (Príomh-Aireach) chosen by Dáil Éireann, and four other Ministers, viz.:

 Minister of Finance (Aireach Airgid),

 Minister of Home Affairs (A. Gnóthaí Dúthchais),

 Minister of Foreign Affairs (A. Gnóthaí Coigcríoch), and

 Minister of Defence (A. Cosanta).

The Prime Minister shall nominate the four others, and shall have power to dismiss them from office.

 (3) Every Minister must be a member of the Dáil, and shall at all times be answerable to the Dáil.

 (4) The names of Ministers must be put before the Dáil for ratification at the first assembly after their nomination by the Prime Minister.

Prime Minister

 (5) The Prime Minister shall hold office as soon as elected and the other Ministers as soon as their appointment is ratified by the Dáil.

 (6) The Dáil shall have power by vote to dismiss the Ministry

or any of the Ministers from office if a written order in the form of a unanimous resolution be presented for that object seven days previously.

Section Three

Every meeting of the Dáil shall be presided over by a Chairman (Ceann Cómhairle) or Vice-Chairman (Ceann Ionaid) chosen by the Dáil for the year. Should the Chairman and Vice-Chairman be absent, the Dáil shall select substitutes or elect a Provisional Chairman (Ceann Cómhairle Sealadach).

Section Four

The Ministry shall receive whatever money it needs, by vote of the Dáil. The Ministry shall be answerable to the Dáil for such moneys, and the accounts shall be audited with regard to the spending of money for the Dáil twice yearly, viz., at Samhain and Bealtaine (November and May). The auditing shall be carried out by an auditor or auditors chosen by the Dáil. No member of the Dáil shall be chosen as auditor.

Section Five

The present is a provisional constitution, and may be altered on a written unanimous order being given to that effect seven days previously.

As approved provisionally at the first meeting of Dáil Éireann, 21 January 1919.

Appendix 13

Declaration of Independence*

'Whereas the Irish People is by right a free people:

'And whereas for seven hundred years the Irish People has never ceased to repudiate and has repeatedly protested in arms against foreign usurpation:

'And whereas English rule in this country is, and always has been, based upon force and fraud and maintained by military occupation against the declared will of the people:

'And whereas the Irish Republic was proclaimed in Dublin on Easter Monday, 1916, by the Irish Republican Army, acting on behalf of the Irish People:

'And whereas the Irish People is resolved to secure and maintain its complete independence in order to promote the common weal, to re-establish justice, to provide for future defence, to ensure peace at home and good will with all nations, and to constitute a national policy based upon the people's will with equal right and equal opportunity for every citizen:

'And whereas at the threshold of a new era in history the Irish electorate has in the general election of December, 1918, seized the first occasion to declare by an overwhelming majority its firm allegiance to the Irish Republic:

'Now, therefore, we, the elected Representatives of the ancient Irish People in National Parliament assembled, do, in the name of the Irish Nation, ratify the establishment of the Irish Republic and pledge ourselves and our people to make this declaration effective by every means at our command:

'We ordain that the elected Representatives of the Irish People alone have power to make laws binding on the people of Ireland, and that the Irish Parliament is the only Parliament to which that people will give its allegiance:

'We solemnly declare foreign government in Ireland to be an invasion of our national right which we will never tolerate, and we demand the evacuation of our country by the English Garrison:

'We claim for our national independence the recognition and support of every free nation in the world, and we proclaim that independence to be a condition precedent to international peace hereafter:

'In the name of the Irish People we humbly commit our destiny to Almighty God Who gave our fathers the courage and determination to persevere through long centuries of a ruthless tyranny, and strong in the justice of the cause which they have handed down to us, we ask His Divine blessing on this the last stage of the struggle we have pledged ourselves to carry through to freedom.'

* English language version – Enacted by the Parliament of the Republic of Ireland at its first meeting, 21 January 1919

Appendix 14

Greeting*

The Nation of Ireland having proclaimed her national independence, calls, through her elected representatives in Parliament assembled in the Irish capital on January 21st, 1919, upon every free nation to support the Irish Republic by recognising Ireland's national status and her right to its vindication at the Peace Congress.

Naturally, the race, the language, the customs and traditions of Ireland are radically distinct from the English. Ireland is one of the most ancient nations in Europe, and she has preserved her national integrity, vigorous and intact, through seven centuries of foreign oppression; she has never relinquished her national rights, and throughout the long era of English usurpation she has in every generation defiantly proclaimed her inalienable right of nationhood down to her last glorious resort to arms in 1916.

Internationally, Ireland is the gateway to the Atlantic; Ireland is the last outpost of Europe towards the west; Ireland is the point upon which great trade routes between east and west converge; her independence is demanded by the Freedom of the Seas; her great harbours must be open to all nations, instead of being the monopoly of England. Today these harbours are empty and idle solely because English policy is determined to retain Ireland as a barren bulwark for English aggrandisement, and the unique geographical position of this island, far from being a benefit and safeguard to Europe and America, is subjected to the purposes of England's policy of world domination.

Ireland today reasserts her historic nationhood the more confidently before the new world emerging from the war, because she believes in freedom and justice as the fundamental principles of international law; because she believes in a frank co-operation between the people for equal rights against the vested privileges of ancient tyrannies; because the permanent peace of Europe can never be secured by perpetuating military dominion for the profit of empire but only by establishing the control of government in every land upon the basis of the free will of a free people, and the existing state of war, between Ireland and England, can never be ended until Ireland is definitely evacuated by the armed forces of England.

For these among other reasons, Ireland – resolutely and irrevocably determined at the dawn of the promised era of self-determination and liberty that she will suffer foreign domination no longer – calls upon every free nation to uphold her national claim to complete independence as an Irish Republic against the arrogant pretensions of England founded in fraud and sustained only by an overwhelming military occupation, and demands to be confronted publicly with England at the Congress of the Nations, that the civilised world having judged between English wrong and Irish right may guarantee to Ireland its permanent support for the maintenance of her national independence.

Greeting – To the Free Nations of the World, read in Irish, French and English at the first meeting of Dáil Éireann, 21 January 1919.

Appendix 15

Republican Army Orders, 1921

Irish Republican Army,
General Headquarters,
Dublin.
22nd June, 1921.

General Orders
Reprisals

1. Brigade Commandants are authorised to answer reprisals against property on the part of the Enemy in the following way: (Where a Division has been formed Brigade Commandants will require to receive formal delegation of authority from their Divisional Commandants.)

2. On every occasion on which the Enemy destroys house property, or house contents, whether alleging military necessity or not, the following counter-reprisals may be taken:

(a) A similar number of houses belonging to the most active enemies of Ireland may be destroyed in the Battalion area in which the original destruction takes place.

(b) An equal number of houses belonging to the most active enemies of Ireland, may, in addition, be destroyed at that point in the Brigade area concerned which may be considered as the centre most strongly occupied by such enemies.

(c) The case should be reported to GHQ with a covering statement of what has been done; and with a view to possible further action.

(d) Where the Enemy persists in taking counter-reprisals, they may be answered in the same way; stopping only when the district concerned has been entirely cleared of active enemies of Ireland.

3. Formal notice shall be served on any person whose house is so destroyed, stating clearly that it is a reprisal because of similar destruction carried out by their military forces; and specifying the particular property for whose destruction it is a reprisal.

4. In any particular case, or in any particular district in which, in addition to such reprisals, it would seem desirable that;

(a) The members of any particular family concerned should be ordered out of the country: or

(b) Have their lands confiscated;

a special report should be submitted.

5. For the purposes of such reprisals no person shall be regarded as enemies of Ireland, whether they may be described locally as Unionist, Orangemen, etc., unless they are actively anti-Irish in their actions.

6. No house shall be selected for destruction or destroyed without the personal approval and permission of the Brigade Commandant.

By Order,
ADJUTANT-GENERAL*

* *Gearóid O'Sullivan succeeded Michael Collins in this position in April 1919. The document probably reflects over-all GHQ thinking, including that of the IRA Chief-of-Staff during the Black and Tan War period, General Richard Mulcahy.*

APPENDIX 16

ARTICLES OF AGREEMENT
Signed on 6 December 1921

1. Ireland shall have the same constitutional status in the Community of Nations known as the British Empire as the Dominion of New Zealand, and the Union of South Africa, with a parliament having powers to make laws for the peace, order and good government of Ireland and an Executive responsible to that Parliament, and shall be styled and known as the Irish Free State.

2. Subject to the provisions hereinafter set out the position of the Irish Free State in relation to the Imperial Parliament and Government and otherwise shall be that of the Dominion of Canada, and the law, practice and constitutional usage governing the relationship of the Crown or the representative of the Crown and of the Imperial Parliament to the Dominion of Canada shall govern their relationship to the Irish Free State.

3. The representative of the Crown in Ireland shall be appointed in like manner as the Governor-General of Canada and in accordance with the practice observed in the making of such appointments.

4. The oath to be taken by Members of the Parliament of the Irish Free State shall be in the following form:

I ... do solemnly swear true faith and allegiance to the Constitution of the Irish Free State as by law established and that I will be faithful to HM King George V, his heirs and successors by law, in virtue of the common citizenship of Ireland with Great Britain and her adherence to and membership of the group of nations forming the British Commonwealth of Nations.

5. The Irish Free State shall assume liability for the service of the Public Debt of the United Kingdom as existing at the date here-

of and towards the payment of war pensions as existing at that date in such proportion as may be fair and equitable, having regard to any just claims on the part of Ireland by way of set-off or counter-claim, the amount of such sums being determined in default of agreement by the arbitration of one or more independent persons being citizens of the British Empire.

6. Until an arrangement has been made between the British and Irish Governments whereby the Irish Free State undertakes her own coastal defence, the defence by sea of Great Britain and Ireland shall be undertaken by His Majesty's Imperial Forces. But this shall not prevent the construction or maintenance by the Government of the Irish Free State of such vessels as are necessary for the protection of the Revenue or the Fisheries.

The foregoing provisions of the Article shall be reviewed at a Conference of Representatives of the British and Irish Government to be held at the expiration of five years from the date hereof with a view to the undertaking by Ireland of a share in her own coastal defence.

7. The government of the Irish Free State shall afford to His Majesty's Imperial Forces: (a) In time of peace such harbour and other facilities as are indicated in the Annex hereto, or such other facilities as may from time to time be agreed between the British Government and the Government of the Irish Free State; and (b) In time of war or of strained relations with a Foreign Power such harbour and other facilities as the British Government may require for the purposes of such defence as aforesaid.

8. With a view to securing the observance of the principle of international limitation of armaments, if the Government of the Irish Free State establishes and maintains a military defence force, the establishments thereof shall not exceed in size such proportion of the military establishments maintained in Great Britain as that which the population of Ireland bears to the population of Great Britain.

9. The ports of Great Britain and the Irish Free State shall be freely open to the ships of the other country on payment of the customary port and other dues.

10. The Government of the Irish Free State agrees to pay fair compensation on terms no less favourable than those accorded by the Act of 1920 to judges, officials, members of Police Forces and other Public Servants who are discharged by it or who retire in consequence of the change of Government effected in pursuance hereof.

Provided that this agreement shall not apply to members of the Auxiliary Police Force or to persons recruited in Great Britain for the Royal Irish Constabulary during the two years next preceding the date hereof. The British Government will assume responsibility for such compensation or pensions as may be payable to any of these excepted persons.

11. Until the expiration of one month from the passing of the Act of Parliament for the ratification of this instrument, the powers of the Parliament and the Government of the Irish Free State shall not be exercisable as respects Northern Ireland and the Provisions of the Government of Ireland Act, 1920, shall so far as they relate to Northern Ireland remain of full force and effect, and no election shall be held for the return of members to serve in the Parliament of the Irish Free State for constituencies in Northern Ireland unless a resolution is passed by both Houses of the Parliament of Northern Ireland in Favour of the holding of such election before the end of the said month.

12. If before the expiration of the said month, an address is presented to His Majesty by both Houses of the Parliament of Northern Ireland to that effect, the powers of the Parliament and Government of the Irish Free State shall no longer extend to Northern Ireland, and the provisions of the Government of Ireland Act 1920 (including those relating to the Council of Ireland) shall so far as they relate to Northern Ireland, continue to be full force and effect,

and this instrument shall have effect subject to the necessary modifications.

Provided that if such an address is so presented a Commission consisting of three persons, one to be appointed by the Government of the Irish State, one to be appointed by the Government of Northern Ireland and one who shall be Chairman to be appointed by the British Government shall determine in accordance with the wishes of the inhabitants, so far as may be compatible with economic and geographic conditions, the boundaries between Northern Ireland and the rest of Ireland and for the purposes of the Government of Ireland Act, 1920, and of this instrument, the boundary of Northern Ireland shall be such as may be determined by such Commission.

13. For the purpose of the last foregoing article, the powers of the Parliament of Southern Ireland under the Government of Ireland Act 1920, to elect members of the Council of Ireland shall after the Parliament of the Irish Free State is constituted be exercised by that Parliament.

14. After the expiration of the said month, if no such address as is mentioned in Article 12 hereof is presented, the Parliament and Government of Northern Ireland shall continue in exercise as respects Northern Ireland the powers conferred on them by the Government of Ireland Act 1920, but the Parliament and Government of the Irish Free State shall in Northern Ireland have in relation to matters in respect of which the Parliament of Northern Ireland had not power to make laws under that Act (including matters which under the said Act within the jurisdiction of the Council of Ireland) the same powers as in the rest of Ireland, subject to such other provisions as may be agreed in manner hereinafter appearing.

15. At any time after the date hereof the Government of Northern Ireland and the provisional Government of Southern Ireland hereinafter constituted may meet for the purpose of discussing the

provisions subject to which the last foregoing article is to operate in the event of no such address as is therein mentioned being presented and those provisions may include:

(a) Safeguards with regard to patronage in Northern Ireland;

(b) Safeguards with regard to the collection of revenue in Northern Ireland;

(c) Safeguards with regard to import and export duties affecting the trade or industry of Northern Ireland;

(d) Safeguards for minorities in Northern Ireland;

(e) The settlement of the financial relations between Northern Ireland and the Irish Free State;

(f) The establishment and powers of a local militia in Northern Ireland and the relation of the Defence Forces of the Irish Free State and of Northern Ireland respectively; and if at any such meeting provisions are agreed to, the same shall have effect as if they were included amongst the provisions subject to which the Powers of the Parliament and Government of the Irish Free State are to be exercisable in Northern Ireland under Article 14 hereof.

16. Neither the Parliament of the Irish Free State nor the Parliament of Northern Ireland shall make any law so as either directly or indirectly to endow any religion or prohibit or restrict the free exercise thereof or give any preference or impose any disability on account of religious belief or religious status or affect prejudicially the right of any child to attend a school receiving public money without attending the religious instruction at the school or make any discrimination as respects state aid between schools under the management of different religious denominations or divert from any religious denomination or any educational institution any of its property except for public utility purposes and on payment of compensation.

17. By way of provisional arrangement for the administration of Southern Ireland during the interval which must elapse between the date hereof and the constitution of a Parliament and

Government of the Irish Free State in accordance therewith, steps shall be taken forthwith for summoning a meeting of members of Parliament elected for constituencies in Southern Ireland since the passing of the Government of Ireland Act, 1920, and for constituting a Provisional Government, and the British Government shall take the steps necessary to transfer to such Provisional Government the powers and machinery requisite for the discharge of its duties, provided that every member of such Provisional Government shall have signified in writing his or her acceptance of this instrument. But this arrangement shall not continue in force beyond the expiration of twelve months from the date hereof.

18. This instrument shall be submitted forthwith by His Majesty's Government for the approval of Parliament and by the Irish signatories to a meeting summoned for the purpose of the members elected to sit in the House of Commons of Southern Ireland, and if approved shall be ratified by the necessary legislation.

On behalf of the British Delegation	On behalf of the Irish Delegation
Signed	Signed
D. Lloyd George	Art Ó Griobhtha
Austen Chamberlain	Micheál Ó Coileáin
Birkenhead	Riobárd Bartún
Winston S. Churchill	Eudhmonn S. Ó Dúgáin
L. Worthington-Evans	Seorsa Ghabháin Uí Dhúbhthaígh
Hamar Greenwood	
Gordon Hewart	

December 6th, 1921

*Note: The word 'Treaty' is not used in this basic document. Note also the requirement in Article 17 that all members of the Provisional Government would have to signify in writing their acceptance 'of this instrument'. See pp. 24–25 on the Pact election.

APPENDIX 17

CRAIG–COLLINS AGREEMENT*

IRELAND

Heads of agreement between the Provisional Government and Government of Northern Ireland:

(1) Peace is today declared.

(2) From today the two Governments undertake to co-operate in every way in their power with a view to the restoration of peaceful conditions in the unsettled areas.

(3)The police in Belfast to be organised in general in accordance with the following conditions:

(1) Special police in mixed districts to be composed half of Catholics and half of Protestants, special arrangements to be made where Catholics or Protestants are living in other districts. All specials not required for this force to be withdrawn to their homes and their arms handed in.

(2) An Advisory Committee, composed of Catholics, to be set up to assist in the selection of Catholic recruits for the Special police.

(3) All police on duty, except the usual secret service, to be in uniform and officially numbered.

(4) All arms and ammunition issued to police to be deposited in barracks in charge of a military or other competent officer when the policeman is not on duty, and an official record to be kept of all arms issued, and of all ammunition issued and used.

(5) Any search for arms to be carried out by police forces composed half of Catholics and half of Protestants, the military rendering any necessary assistance.

(4) A court to be constituted for the trial without jury of persons charged with serious crime, the Court to consist of the Lord Chief Justice and one of the Lords Justices of Appeal of Northern Ireland. Any person committed for trial for a serious crime to be tried by that court:

(a) if he so requests, or

(b) if the Attorney-General for Northern Ireland so directs.

Serious crime should be taken to mean any offence punishable with death, penal servitude, or imprisonment for a term exceeding six months. The Government of Northern Ireland will take steps for passing the legislation necessary to give effect to this Article.

(5) A Committee to be set up in Belfast of equal numbers Catholic and Protestant with an independent Chairman, preferably Catholic and Protestant alternately in successive weeks, to hear and investigate complaints as to intimidation, outrages, etc., such Committee to have direct access to the heads of the Government. The local Press to be approached with a view to inserting only such reports of disturbances, etc., as shall have been considered and communicated by this committee.

(6) IRA activity to cease in the Six Counties, and thereupon the method of organising the special police in the Six Counties outside Belfast shall proceed as speedily as possible upon lines similar to those agreed to for Belfast.

(7) During the month immediately following the passing into law of the Bill confirming the constitution of the Free State (being the month within which the Northern Parliament is to exercise its option) and before any address in accordance with Article 12 of the Treaty is presented there shall be a further meeting between the signatories to this agreement with a view to ascertaining:

(a) Whether means can be devised to secure the unity of Ireland.

(b) Failing this, whether agreement can be arrived at on the boundary question otherwise than by recourse to the Boundary Commission outlined in Article 12 of the Treaty.

(8) The return to their homes of persons who have been expelled to be secured by the respective Governments, the advice of the Committee mentioned in Article 5 to be sought in cases of difficulty.

(9) In view of the special conditions consequent on the political situation in Belfast and neighbourhood, the British Government will submit to Parliament a vote not exceeding £500,000 for the Ministry of Labour of Northern Ireland to be expended exclusively on relief work, one-third for the benefit of Roman Catholics and two-thirds for the benefit of Protestants. The Northern signatories agree to use every effort to secure the restoration of the expelled workers, and wherever this proves impracticable at the moment owing to trade depression, they will be afforded employment on the relief works referred to in this article so far as the one-third limit will allow. Protestant ex-service men to be given first preference in respect to the two-thirds of the said fund.

(10) The two Governments shall in cases agreed upon between the signatories arrange for the release of political prisoners in prison for offences before the date hereof. No offences committed after March 31st, 1922, shall be open to consideration.

(11) The two Governments unite in appealing to all concerned to refrain from inflammatory speeches and to exercise restraint in the interests of peace.

Signed on behalf of the Provisional Government:
Micheál Ó Coileáin, E. S. Ó Dúgáin, Caoimhghin Ó hUigín, Art Ó Gríobhtha

Signed on behalf of the Government of Northern Ireland:
James Craig, Londonderry, E. M. Archdale

Countersigned on behalf of the British Government:
Winston S. Churchill, L. Worthington-Evans

* *Signed on 30 March 1922.*

Appendix 18

Óglaigh na hÉireann GHQ Staff, October 1917 – July 1921

Any overview of the Irish independence struggle, post 1916, must take account of the increase in popular agitation, and the new political abilities of a re-organised Sinn Féin party, following the Sinn Féin Ardfheis in October 1917. It would be unrealistic to ignore the 'dual purpose' strategy of Irish Republicans in those years, in particular the re-organisation, expansion and training of the Volunteers, much of it in secret. Most of it was pioneered by the secret IRB networks built up in the prison camps the British opened after the 1916 Rising. The entire national leadership sought the first possible opportunity for the democratic endorsement of their Republican separatist programme, and they received this at the December 1918 general election. Sinn Féin proceeded to establish Dáil Éireann and openly challenged Britain's right to rule in Ireland by taking over areas of government, launching a National Loan, establishing Sinn Féin courts, getting control of over 80% of the local authorities, and getting these to pledge their loyalty to the government of the Republic rather than to the British. They made diplomatic and publicity efforts abroad to get international recognition for the newly-declared independent Republic. The British response was not only negative but brutal. Black and Tans and 'specialist' Auxiliary forces were the answer of the British government to Ireland's claim to rule her own affairs, as had clearly been endorsed through the ballot box – a British ballot box as it happens. Into this dual-power situation, where two sides claimed to be the legitimate government of Ireland, stepped the Irish Volunteers, committed to the Dáil and the Republic as Óglaigh na hÉireann, the Irish Republican Army. These were voluntary guerrillas and flying columns whose job it was to defend the Republic and protect the rights of those who had freely voted for it.

Any consideration of the way the army split after the Treaty and fought each other in the Civil War should pay special attention to the IRA General Headquarters, and the personalities who operated there from 1917 to 1921. The best account of this fascinating 'management chart' of IRA General Headquarters, that I am aware of, appears in the book *Cathal Brugha* by the late Tomás Ó Dochartaigh (Brugha's nephew). I reprint a summary of his findings and sources used here.

The original GHQ staff layout covers the period from the Sinn Féin Ardfheis in October 1917 to May 1918, when the British threat to introduce conscription became a huge popular issue. *(Column A)*

Changes were introduced in May 1918, with the appointment of Richard Mulcahy as Assistance Chief-of-Staff, the arrest of Seán McGarry and Michael Staines, and a general increase in activity arising from the conscription threat. *(Column B)*

Changes were made again in April 1919, as a result of the appointment of Cathal Brugha as Minister for Defence by the Dáil, and because it was decided to wage a war of a general but unique guerrilla nature on the British. Richard Mulcahy became Deputy Defence Minister and Chief of Staff and, as such, was at the heart of GHQ activity directing the war against the Black and Tans and the Auxiliaries throughout the country. This war increased in intensity and viciousness up until December 1920, when further changes were made. *(Column C)*

Changes in GHQ were necessary in December 1920, mainly because of the murder, following their capture on Bloody Sunday (21 November 1920) along with Conor Clune, of Richard McKee and Peadar Clancy, Commandant and Vice-Commandant respectively of the IRA in the Dublin area. *(Column D)* This (fourth) line-out remained substantially intact until the Truce in July 1921, although Rory O'Connor, Director of Engineering who had been given additional duties as Officer in Charge of Operations in Britain, was arrested in May 1921.

GHQ full-time or semi-full-time staff never exceeded more than 15 or 16 key persons and many of these people had many other responsibilities as well – including ministries in the Dáil and the work of Dáil Éireann itself.

When the Articles of Agreement or Treaty was signed on 6 December 1921 GHQ, like Sinn Féin and indeed the entire IRA, was split. Defence Minister Cathal Brugha, a member of the cabinet, was one of the most vehement opponents of the compromise, along with President De Valera and Austin Stack, Minister for Home Affairs. On the other side, the three members of the cabinet who had signed in London, Arthur Griffith, Minister for Foreign Affairs, Michael Collins, Minister for Finance, and Robert Barton, Minister for Economic Affairs, were committed to recommending the Articles of Agreement to the Dáil, even if they, and indeed the two other members of the delegation, Éamonn Duggan, TD, and George Gavan Duffy, TD, had serious reservations. Barton's reservations troubled him so much that within a few months he joined the anti-Treaty side and was lodged in Mountjoy Jail, in the summer of 1922.

The seventh member of the cabinet, William T. Cosgrave, Minister for Local Government, who had been a supporter of Arthur Griffith and Sinn Féin from its foundation in 1905, but unlike Griffith had taken arms, without democratic mandate, when the Irish Republic was first declared at Easter 1916, seemed undecided at first. He eventually sided with Griffith and Collins. There were rumours that some members of the IRA proposed to arrest the Treaty delegation when they landed back in Dún Laoghaire, and charge them with disobedience – or even treason against the Republican government.

If you include Defence Minister Brugha and Oscar Traynor OC Dublin Brigade of the IRA, as ex-officio members of the GHQ staff, the breakdown on the Treaty was nine for and three against. If, on the other hand, you calculate the GHQ staff total as being thirteen rather than fifteen, then the breakdown was nine pro-Treaty and four against.

The IRA Chief-of-Staff, Richard Mulcahy, who had borne a lot of the burdens in the Black and Tan period, and who probably had a more realistic estimate of the real capacity of the active service units than most, was pro-Treaty. He never said that he liked the Treaty conditions or limitations, and indicated at least initially, that he would continue to serve as a soldier in whatever position was available if the Dáil rejected what was on offer. Unlike De Valera and Brugha, Mulcahy was a member of the secret IRB, then headed up by Michael Collins. Mulcahy's views carried weight with the other IRB men in the field, as well as with colleagues in GHQ. But because of his actions in pursuit of victory in the Civil War it is worth placing on record what he had to say when he spoke in the Dáil debate on the Treaty just before Christmas, on 22 December 1921: 'What we are looking for here is not arguments but alternatives. None of us want this Treaty. None of us want the crown. None of us want the representatives of the crown. None of us want our harbours occupied by enemy forces; and none of us want what is said to be partition; and we want no arguments against any of these things ... I personally see no alternative to the acceptance of the Treaty ... As to our ports, we are not in a position of force, either military or otherwise, to drive the enemy from our ports. We have not – those on whom the responsibility has been for doing such things – we have not been able to drive the enemy from anything but from a fairly good-sized police barracks. We have suffered a defeat.'

Obviously this negative view from behind the Chief-of-Staff's desk in GHQ was not shared by the Flying Columns in the field, especially in the south and to a lesser degree in the west, north-west, Meath, north midlands and south Ulster. But it did have an impact on GHQ where some eight members of the senior staff opted for the Treaty. These included Collins, Director of Intelligence, whose precise relationship with Mulcahy was always problematic given that Collins had his own small squad of IRB hit-men who were not formally commissioned Volunteers, and were directed by and responsible to Collins for 'special tasks' like the Bloody Sunday assassinations. Those who sided with Mulcahy were:

J. J. O'Connell, Assistant Chief-of-Staff
Eoin O'Duffy, Deputy Chief-of-Staff
Gearóid O'Sullivan, Adjutant-General Secretary
Seán MacMahon, Quartermaster General
Éamon Price, Director of Organisation
Emmet Dalton, Director of Training
Piaras Béaslaí, Director of Publicity and Editor, *An tÓglach*

The four others, apart from Brugha and Traynor, in GHQ who opposed the Treaty were:

Rory O'Connor, Director of Engineering
Seán Russell, Director of Munitions
Liam Mellows, Director of Purchasing
Jim O'Donovan, Director of Chemicals

Let us now take a general look at the GHQ management chart – based largely on the research of the late Tomás Ó Dochartaigh, in the four periods outlined above under A, B, C, D.

	A [note 2] Oct 1917–May 1918	B [note 3] May 1918–April 1919	C [note 4] April 1919–Dec 1920	D [note 5] Dec 1920–July 1921
Minister for Defence	—	—	Cathal Brugha	Cathal Brugha
Chief-of-Staff	Cathal Brugha	Cathal Brugha	Richard Mulcahy	Richard Mulcahy
Assistant Chief-of-Staff	None	Richard Mulcahy	None	J. J. O'Connell
Deputy Chief-of-Staff	None	None	None	Eoin O'Duffy
Secretary/Adjutant General	Seán McGarry (Sec. Executive of Irish Volunteers)	Michael Collins (Temporary Adjutant General)	Gearóid O'Sullivan Adjutant General	Gearóid O'Sullivan
Quartermaster General/ Director of Equipment	Michael Staines Director of Equipment	Michael Collins (Temporary Quartermaster General)	Seán MacMahon (Quartermaster General)	Seán MacMahon
Director of Organisation	Michael Collins	Diarmuid O'Hegarty	Diarmuid O'Hegarty (Éamon Price, Assistant)	Éamon Price
Director of Communications	Diarmaid Lynch	-	*(Incorporated into the duties of the Director of Organisation)*	*(Incorporated into the duties of the Director of Organisation)*
Director of Training	Michael Collins	M. W. O'Reilly	See Note 1	Emmet Dalton
Director of Engineering	Rory O'Connor*	Rory O'Connor	Rory O'Connor	Rory O'Connor
Director of Intelligence	-	Éamonn Duggan	Michael Collins	Michael Collins
Director of Munitions	-	-	Peadar Clancy	Seán Russell
Director of Purchasing	-	-	-	Liam Mellows
Director of Chemicals	-	-	-	Jim O'Donovan
OC Dub lin Brigade	Richard Mulcahy	Richard McKee	Richard McKee	Oscar Traynor
OC Campaign in Britain	-	-	-	Rory O'Connor (Arrested May 1921)
Editor An tÓglach	-	Piaras Béaslaí	Piaras Béaslaí	Piaras Béaslaí

* Though the actual date is uncertain it seems Rory O'Connor was on GHQ Engineering staff from the outset [see note 2].

Notes

1 Originally M. W. O'Reilly wrote *Training Notes* for *An tÓglach*. Full-time Training Officers and Senior Training staff in Dublin attended courses, and these were extended to the rest of the country from August 1919. These courses were under the direction of Richard McKee, but the selection of Training Agents (Timirí Oiliúna) was under the direction of the Chief-of-Staff, or his Deputy.

2 The first munitions factories in Dublin were established by Richard McKee and it is presumed he acted as Director of Munitions until Peadar Clancy was appointed in the autumn of 1920. Clancy was only a few weeks in the position. Both he and McKee (and Conor Clune from Clare) were battered to death in Dublin Castle following Bloody Sunday on 20 November 1920.

3 These changes were prompted by the appointment of Richard Mulcahy as Assistant Chief-of-Staff, the arrest of Seán McGarry and Michael Staines and increased activity arising from the British threat to apply conscription into the British army to Ireland.

4 These changes came about because of the appointment of Cathal Brugha as Minister for Defence, responsible to the Republican government in the First Dáil Éireann, and the pursuit of the war against the British. Mulcahy assumed duties as Assistant Defence Minister as well as full-time Chief-of-Staff from then on.

5 These changes were necessitated because of the deaths of McKee and Clancy and because the Black and Tan war had intensified considerably in the second half of 1920.

Bibliography

Andrews, C. S., *Dublin Made Me*, Cork & Dublin 1979

Béaslaí, Piaras, *Michael Collins and the Making of a New Ireland*, London 1926

Blake, Frances Mary, *The Irish Civil War*, Information on Ireland, London 1986

Collins, Stephen, *The Cosgrave Legacy*, Dublin 1997

Curran, Joseph M., *The Birth of the Irish Free State 1921–23*, Alabama 1980

Deasy, Liam, *Brother Against Brother*, Cork & Dublin, reprinted 1998

Doherty, Gabriel & Keogh, Dermot (Eds), *Michael Collins and the Making of the Irish State*, Cork & Dublin 1998

Eleven Galway Martyrs, Tuam Workhouse Commemoration Committee 1985

Garvin, Tom, *1922 The Birth of Irish Democracy*, Dublin 1996

Harrington, Niall C., *Kerry Landing*, Dublin 1992

Hopkinson, Michael, *Green Against Green*, Dublin 1988

MacAonghusa, Proinsias, *Ros Muc agus Cogadh na Saoirse*, Baile Átha Cliath 1992

Macardle, Dorothy, *The Irish Republic*, London 1968

– *Tragedies of Kerry*, Dublin 1924

MacEoin, Uinseann (Ed.), *Survivors*, Dublin 1987

Maher, Jim, *Harry Boland*, Cork & Dublin 1998

Manning, Maurice, *The Courage to Succeed*, Dublin 1983

Mansergh, Nicholas, *The Unresolved Question*, Yale 1991

– *The Irish Free State: Its Government and Politics*, Cambridge 1934

Mansergh, Diana (Ed.), *Nationalism and Independence*, Cork 1997

Maye, Brian, *Arthur Griffith*, Dublin 1997

Mitchell, Arthur, *Revolutionary Government in Ireland*, Dublin 1995

Neeson, Eoin, *The Civil War in Ireland*, Cork & Dublin 1966

Nelson, Justin, *Michael Collins, The Final Days*, Dublin 1997

Ó Brádaigh, Ruairí, *Dílseacht, The Story of General Tom Maguire*, Dublin 1998

Ó Ceallaigh, Seán T., *Seán T. II*. Baile Átha Cliath 1972

O'Connor, Frank, *The Big Fellow*, London 1969

Ó Dochartaigh, Tomás, *Cathal Brugha*, Baile Átha Cliath 1969

O'Donoghue, Florence, *No Other Law*, Dublin 1952

Ó Gadhra, Nollaig, *An Chéad Dáil Éireann 1919–21*, Baile Átha Cliath 1989

– *Guth an Phobail*, Baile Átha Cliath 1984

O'Hegarty, P. S., *A History of Ireland Under the Union 1801 to 1922*, London 1952

Ó Luing, Seán, *Art Ó Gríobhtha*, Baile Átha Cliath 1953

O'Malley, Edward, *Memories of a Mayoman*, Baile Átha Cliath 1991

Ó Néill, Tomás P. & Ó Fiannachta, Pádraig, *De Valera II*, Baile Átha Cliath 1970

Ó Snodaigh, Pádraig, *Ón Droichead go dtí an Duibheagán*, Baile Átha Cliath 1997

O'Sullivan, Donal, *The Irish Free State and Its Senate*, London 1940.

Ring, Jim, *Erskine Childers*, London 1996

Sceilg (Seán Ua Ceallaigh), *Cathal Brugha*, Baile Átha Cliath 1942

Taylor Rex, *Michael Collins*, London 1958

Valiulis, Maryann Gialanella, *General Richard Mulcahy and the Founding of the Irish Free State*, Dublin 1992

Walker, Brian M. (Ed.), *Parliamentary Election Results in Ireland 1918–1992*, Dublin 1992

White, Terence De Vere, *Kevin O'Higgins*, London 1948

INDEX

188